2 0

MW01602152

POCKET PRICE GUIDE

AMERICAN FLYER®

AND OTHER S GAUGE MANUFACTURERS

Editor: Kent J. Johnson

KALMBACH BOOKS

 Published by Kalmbach Publishing Co., 21027 Crossroads Circle, Waukesha, WI 53186.

Manufactured in the United States of America

Sixteenth Edition

For more information, visit our website at http://books.kalmbach.com

Cover design: Kristi Ludwig
Cover photo: Model provided by Mike Hilbert. No. 350 royal blue 4-6-2 Pacific steam locomotive produced in 1948 and 1950 by A. C. Gilbert Company.

CONTENTS

NUMERICAL LISTINGS

CATALOGS AND MANUALS

INTRODUCTION

This revised Pocket Price Guide lists all major AMERICAN FLYER S GAUGE items built by the A. C. Gilbert Company, Lionel Trains, Inc., or Lionel LLC. This guide also lists ready-to-run items from two contemporary S gauge manufacturers, American Models and S-Helper Service.

The values quoted for American Flyer items are indicative of the most common variety. Rare varieties, many of which are included here, are sometimes worth considerably more. Some newly manufactured items made by Lionel LLC, American Models, or S-Helper Service may not have well-established prices; they are either marked "CP" for current production or valued at retail price.

Dates cited herein are the cataloged dates. If there is no catalog date, production dates are listed if they are known. American Flyer often printed "Built Dates" on its equipment. Note, however, that these dates may or may not coincide with the actual catalog dates or production dates.

For additional information on all S gauge items, please consult these comprehensive volumes: *Greenberg's Guide to American Flyer S Gauge, Volumes I, II, and III.*

Notes to Collectors

We receive numerous inquiries as to whether or not a particular piece is a "good value." This book will help you answer that question; however, there is NO substitute for experience in the marketplace.

WE STRONGLY RECOMMEND THAT NOVICES DO NOT MAKE MAJOR PURCHASES WITHOUT THE ASSISTANCE OF FRIENDS WHO HAVE EXPERIENCE IN BUYING AND SELLING TRAINS.

Train values in this Pocket Price Guide are based on prices obtained at large train meets from 1999 and from private transactions reported by our review panel. These values are meant to serve only as a guide to collectors—they are an averaged reflection of prices across the country to be used by train collectors nationwide. Values in your area may be consistent with values in this guide, or they may be higher or lower depending upon the relative availability or scarcity of any particular item. Economic conditions in your area may also affect these values. If you are selling a train to a person planning to resell it, you will NOT obtain the values reported in this book. Rather, you may expect to receive about 50 percent of these prices. For your item to be of interest to such a buyer, it must be purchased for considerably less than the price listed here. But if you are dealing with another collector, values may be expected to be more consistent with the guide. Also, we have observed that a considerable amount of action at train meets usually occurs in the first hour. The items that do not sell in the first hour usually have a higher price tag, but sometimes there is a willingness of some sellers to bargain over the marked price.

From our studies of train prices, it appears that mail-order prices for used trains are generally higher than those obtained at train meets (those listed in this book), considering the cost and effort of producing and distributing a price list as well as packing and shipping items. Mail-order items generally sell at prices above those listed in this book.

We are constantly striving to improve Greenberg's Pocket Price Guides. If you find any missing items or detect any misinformation, please, by all means, write to us. If you have any recommendations for improving a listing, we would like to hear from you. Send your comments, new information, or corrections to:

Editor—American Flyer Pocket Guide (10-8600)
Books Division
Kalmbach Publishing Co.
21027 Crossroads Circle
P.O. Box 1612
Waukesha, WI 53187-1612

CONDITIONS

This Pocket Price Guide lists prices for Gilbert production pieces in GOOD and EXCELLENT condition, and Lionel production pieces in NEW condition. Prices for restored pieces fall between Good and Excellent, depending on the item. Gilbert paper is listed in GOOD and EXCELLENT condition, while Lionel paper is listed as EXCELLENT and NEW. New pieces bring a substantial premium over Excellent pieces. Fair pieces bring substantially less than Good and Excellent pieces.

In the toy train field there is a great deal of concern with exterior appearance and less concern with operation. If operation is important to you, you should ask the seller if the train runs. If the seller indicates that he does not know whether the equipment operates, you should test it. Most train meets provide test tracks for this purpose.

Trains and related items are usually classified by condition.

The categories used here are:

- **FAIR**—well-scratched, chipped, dented, rusted, or warped.
- **GOOD**—scratched, dirty, with small dents.
- **VERY GOOD**—few scratches, no dents or rust; very clean.
- **EXCELLENT**—minute scratches or nicks; exceptionally clean.
- **LIKE NEW**—free of blemishes, nicks, or scratches; original condition throughout, with vibrant colors; only faint signs of handling or use; price includes original box.
- **NEW**—brand new, absolutely unmarred, all original and unused, with no evidence of being handled. Packaged in original box; complete with all original paperwork.
- **RESTORED**—professionally refinished to a color that very closely approximates the original finish. Trim and ornamentation are present and are in Like New condition. The finish appears in Like New condition.

- **REPRODUCTION**—a product intended to closely resemble the original item. It may or may not be marked as such, but should be so marked. Reproductions are currently available for many desirable items.

- **CP** (Current Production) means that the item is currently advertised, manufactured, or available from retail stores.

- **NRS** (No Recorded Sales) means the editors did not have sufficient information to establish a price. The item may be very scarce and bring a substantial premium over items in its general class, or it may be relatively common but unnoticed. Usually NRS listings occur when an item is first reported, although we are still discovering relatively common variations that have not been previously reported. If you have information about the value of an NRS item, please write to us. Note: An item labeled NRS does not always secure a high price. Extreme caution is advised when purchasing any NRS item for a substantial sum.

- **NM** (Not Manufactured) means that the item may have been cataloged or otherwise advertised, but it was not produced.

- **(#)** Numbers that have been put in parentheses by us do not appear on the actual items.

- **[#]** means decorations that make this item unique were not done by Lionel.

- **No Number** means the item may have lettering but lacks an item number.

- **(no letters)** means the item has no lettering or number on the car.

- * means excellent reproductions have been made.

GILBERT PRODUCTION
1946–1966

American Flyer Circus Coach See (649)
American Flyer Circus Flatcar See (643)
Borden's Flatcar Pike Master couplers See (24575)
Buffalo Hunt Gondola, *63* 4 14 _____
C&NWRWY 42597 w/ link couplers See (628)
C&NWRWY 42597 w/ knuckle couplers See (928) or 934
Freight Ahead Caboose, *63* 3 10 _____
G. Fox & Co. See (633F)
Keystone See (24067)
New Haven w/ pipes, Pike Master couplers See (24564)
Pennsylvania See (24130)
Rocket Launcher and USM See (25056)
Simmons See (24420)
Undecorated Flatcar body (See 24575)
Virginian See (632)
Washington See (21089)

1	25-watt Transformer, *49–52*	1	3	_____
1	35-watt Transformer, *56*	4	8	_____
1A	40-watt Transformer, *57 u*	3	8	_____
1½	45-watt Transformer, *53*	1	5	_____
1½	50-watt Transformer, *54–55*	1	5	_____
1½B	50-watt Transformer, *56*	1	5	_____
2	75-watt Transformer, *47–53*	2	7	_____
2B	75-watt Transformer, *47–48*	3	11	_____
3	50-watt Transformer, *46 u*	2	6	_____
4B	100-watt Transformer, *49–56*	11	24	_____
5	50-watt Transformer, *46*	2	6	_____
5A	50-watt Transformer, *46*	2	6	_____
5B	50-watt Transformer, *46*	3	6	_____
6	75-watt Transformer, *46*	1	5	_____
6A	75-watt Transformer, *46*	1	5	_____
7	75-watt Transformer, *46 u*	2	8	_____
7B	75-watt Transformer, *46*	2	8	_____
8B	100-watt Transformer, *46–52*	10	23	_____
9B	150-watt Transformer, *46*	17	32	_____
10	DC Inverter, *46*	7	19	_____
11	Circuit Breaker, *46*	3	11	_____
12B	250-watt Transformer, *46–52*	27	80	_____
13	Circuit Breaker, *52–55*	4	8	_____
14	Rectiformer, *47, 49*	8	26	_____
15	Rectifier, *48–52*	6	23	_____
15B	110-watt Transformer, *53*	13	33	_____

		Good	Exc	Cond/$
16	Rectiformer, *50*	10	32	_____
16B	190-watt Transformer, *53*	30	70	_____
16B	175-watt Transformer, *54–56*	25	65	_____
16C	35-watt Transformer, *58*	7	19	_____
17B	190-watt Transformer, *52*	32	75	_____
18	Filter, *50 u*		NRS	_____
18B	175-watt Transformer, *54–56*	25	75	_____
18B	190-watt Transformer, *53*	27	80	_____
19B	300-watt Transformer, *52–55*	50	115	_____
20	See (247)20			
21	Imitation Grass, *49–50*	16	26	_____
21A	Imitation Grass, *51–56*	16	26	_____
22	Scenery Gravel, *49–56*	12	20	_____
23	Artificial Coal, *49–56*	12	20	_____
24	Rainbow Wire, *49–56*	3	9	_____
25	Smoke Cartridge, *47–56*	4	11	_____
26	Service Kit, *52–56*	5	21	_____
27	Track Cleaning Fluid, *52–56*	2	7	_____
28	Track Ballast, *50*	5	12	_____
28A	Track Ballast, *51–53*	5	13	_____
29	Imitation Snow, *50*	47	105	_____
29A	Imitation Snow, *51–53*	49	110	_____
30	Highway Signs, *49–52*	38	140	_____
30	See (247)30			
30B	300-watt Transformer, *53–56*	70	155	_____
31	Railroad Signs, *49–50*	70	195	_____
31A	Railroad Signs, *51–52*	70	195	_____
32	City Street Equipment, *49–50*	50	175	_____
32A	Park set, *51*	50	185	_____
33	Passenger and Train Figure set, *51–52*	65	200	_____
34	Railway Figure set, *53*	95	720	_____
35	Brakeman w/ lantern, *50–52*	85	160	_____
40	See (247)40			
40	Smoke set, *53–56*	3	5	_____
50	District School, *53–54*	47	155	_____
50	See (247)50			
55	See (240)55			
65	See (245)65			
88	See (210)88			
100	Step Display, *48*	55	220	_____
100	Universal Lock-on		NRS	_____
160	Station Platform, *53*	125	290	_____

		Good	Exc	Cond/$
161	Bungalow, *53*	90	190	_____
162	Factory, *53*	75	240	_____
163	Flyerville Station, *53*	95	170	_____
164	Red Barn, *53*	95	385	_____
165	Grain Elevator, *53*	50	210	_____
166	Church, *53*	95	310	_____
167	Town hall, *53*	100	340	_____
168	Hotel, *53*	100	295	_____
234	See (21)234			
247	Tunnel, *46–48*	22	38	_____
248	Tunnel, *46–48*	22	38	_____
249	Tunnel, *47–56*	15	36	_____
263	PRR 0-6-0 Switcher, *57*		NM	_____
270	News and Frank Stand, *52–53*	44	110	_____
271	Three-Piece "Whistle Stop" set, *52–53*	55	140	_____
	1) Waiting Station	20	49	_____
	2) Refreshment Booth	20	49	_____
	3) Newsstand	20	49	_____
272	Glendale Station and Newsstand, *52–53*	50	150	_____
273	Suburban Railroad Station, *52–53*	50	150	_____
274	Harbor Junction Freight Station, *52–53*	50	155	_____
275	Eureka Diner, *52–53*	40	160	_____
282	CNW 4-6-2 Pacific, *52–53*			
	(A) "American Flyer", *52*	36	70	_____
	(B) w/ coal pusher, *53*	40	80	_____
283	CNW 4-6-2 Pacific, *54–57*	29	85	_____
285	CNW 4-6-2 Pacific, *52*	42	130	_____
287	CNW 4-6-2 Pacific, *54*	20	80	_____
289	CNW 4-6-2 Pacific, *56 u*	80	250	_____
290	American Flyer 4-6-2 Pacific, *49–51*	25	70	_____
293	NYNH&H 4-6-2 Pacific, *53–58*			
	(A) Reverse in tender, *53–57*	47	115	_____
	(B) Reverse in cab, *57 u*	80	160	_____
295	American Flyer 4-6-2 Pacific, *51*	80	210	_____
296	NYNH&H 4-6-2 Pacific, *55 u*	85	315	_____
299	Reading 4-4-2 Atlantic, *54 u*	41	145	_____
300	Reading 4-4-2 Atlantic, *46–47, 52*			
	(A) "Reading", *46–47*	20	60	_____
	(B) Other variations, *47, 52*	15	46	_____
300 AC	Reading 4-4-2 Atlantic, *49–50*	15	44	_____
301	Reading 4-4-2 Atlantic, *53*	15	45	_____

		Good	Exc	Cond/$
302	RL 4-4-2 Atlantic (mv), *48, 51–53*			
	(A) Smoke in tender			
	(B) Smoke in boiler	15	50	_____
	(C) Plastic	15	50	_____
302AC	Reading Lines 4-4-2 Atlantic (mv), *48, 51–52*	17	55	_____
303	Reading 4-4-2 Atlantic, *54–56*	15	55	_____
305	Reading 4-4-2, *51*		NM	_____
307	Reading 4-4-2 Atlantic, *54–57*	15	41	_____
308	Reading 4-4-2 Atlantic, *56*	25	90	_____
310	PRR 4-6-2 Pacific, *46–48*	44	140	_____
312	PRR 4-6-2 Pacific (mv), *46, 48, 51–52*			
	(A) "Pennsylvania", s-i-t, *46*	60	150	_____
	(B) Other variations	60	125	_____
312AC	PRR 4-6-2 Pacific, *49–51*	60	130	_____
313	PRR 4-6-2 Pacific, *55–56*	60	205	_____
314AW	PRR 4-6-2 Pacific, *49–50*	75	280	_____
315	PRR 4-6-2 Pacific, *52*	60	195	_____
316	PRR 4-6-2 Pacific, *53–54*	65	220	_____
320	NYC 4-6-4 Hudson, *46–47*	60	165	_____
321	NYC 4-6-4 Hudson, *46–47*	50	205	_____
322	NYC 4-6-4 Hudson, *46–50*			
	(A) "New York Central", *46*	41	165	_____
	(B) "American Flyer Lines", *47–50*	39	155	_____
322AC	NYC 4-6-4 Hudson, *49–50*	41	145	_____
324AC	NYC 4-6-4 Hudson, *50*	60	190	_____
325AC	NYC 4-6-4 Hudson, *51*	55	165	_____
K325	NYC 4-6-4 Hudson, *52*			
	(A) Early coupler riveted to truck	155	315	_____
	(B) Other variations	50	155	_____
326	NYC 4-6-4 Hudson, *53–57*			
	(A) Small motor	60	205	_____
	(B) Large motor	90	235	_____
332	Union Pacific 4-8-4, Northern, *46–49*			
	(A) AC, "Union Pacific" s-i-t, *46*			
	(B) AC "American Flyer Lines", *47–48*	140	380	_____
	(C) DC "American Flyer Lines", *48–49*	140	380	_____
	(D) DC silver lettering, *47*	1100	2450	_____
332AC	Union Pacific 4-8-4 Northern, *50–51*	155	380	_____
332DC	Union Pacific 4-8-4 Northern, *49*	140	465	_____
334DC	Union Pacific 4-8-4 Northern, *50*	160	480	_____
K335	Union Pacific 4-8-4 Northern, *52*	125	400	_____

		Good	Exc	Cond/$
336	Union Pacific 4-8-4 Northern, *53–56*			
	(A) Small motor	135	440	_____
	(B) Large motor	140	445	_____
342	NKP 0-8-0 Switcher, *46–48, 52*			
	(A) "Nickel Plate Road" s-i-t, *46*			
	(B) "American Flyer Lines" s-i-t, *47*	115	420	_____
	(C) Same as (B), but DC	120	470	_____
	(D) "American Flyer Lines" s-i-b, *48*	95	365	_____
	(E) "American Flyer", *52*	100	395	_____
342AC	NKP 0-8-0 Switcher, *49–51*	90	295	_____
342DC	NKP 0-8-0 Switcher, *48–50*	95	290	_____
343	NKP 0-8-0 Switcher, *53–58*			
	(A) Reverse in tender, *53–54*	110	360	_____
	(B) Reverse on motor, *54, 56*	125	395	_____
346	NKP 0-8-0 Switcher, *55*	225	630	_____
350	Royal Blue 4-6-2 Pacific (mv), *48, 50*			
	(A) Wire handrails, *48*	47	140	_____
	(B) Cast handrails, *50*	40	130	_____
353	AF Circus 4-6-2 Pacific, *50–51*	130	460	_____
354	Silver Bullet 4-6-2 Pacific, *54*	65	200	_____
355	CNW Baldwin, *56–57*			
	(A) Unpainted green plastic	70	145	_____
	(B) Green-painted plastic	120	300	_____
356	Silver Bullet 4-6-2 Pacific, *53*			
	(A) Chrome	60	200	_____
	(B) Satin-silver paint			
360/361	Santa Fe PA/PB, *50–51*			
	(A) Chromed, *50*	70	280	_____
	(B) Chromed w/ handrails, *50*	110	510	_____
	(C) Silver-painted, *51*	65	210	_____
360/364	Santa Fe PA/PB, *50–51*			
	(A) Silver-painted, "Santa Fe", *50*	70	220	_____
	(B) Other variations			
360/361/360	SP PA/PB/PA Cutout Pilots, u		NRS	_____
370	GM AF GP-7, *50–53*			
	(A) w/ link coupler bars	65	170	_____
	(B) w/ knuckle couplers	65	175	_____
371	GM AF GP-7, *54*	105	260	_____
372	Union Pacific GP-7, *55–57*			
	(A) "Built by Gilbert"	125	265	_____
	(B) "Made by American Flyer"	135	320	_____

		Good	Exc	Cond/$
374/375	Texas & Pacific GP-7, *55*			
	(A) Sheet metal frame	190	480	_____
	(B) Die-cast frame	175	445	_____
375	GM AF GP-7, *53*	680	1700	_____
377/378	Texas & Pacific GP-7, *56–57*	190	580	_____
(405)	Silver Streak PA, *52*	90	280	_____
440	Lamp	2	6	_____
441	Lamp	2	6	_____
442	Lamp	2	6	_____
443	Lamp	2	6	_____
444	Lamp	2	6	_____
450	Track Terminal, *46–48*	2	6	_____
451	Lamp	2	6	_____
452	Lamp	2	6	_____
453	Lamp, *46–48*			
	(A) One bulb	2	6	_____
	(B) Three bulbs	2	6	_____
460	Bulbs, *51, 53–54*	30	85	_____
461	Lamp	2	8	_____
466	Comet, PA, *53–55*			
	(A) Chromed, *53*	85	215	_____
	(B) Silver-painted, decal, *54–55*	70	205	_____
	(C) Silver-painted, w/ heat-stamped lett.	90	255	_____
467	Comet PB, *55**		NRS	_____
470/471/473	SF PA/PB/PA, *53–57*			
	(A) Chromed, *53*	140	460	_____
	(B) Silver-painted, *54–57*	115	380	_____
	(C) Silver-painted, integral steps	250	580	_____
472	Santa Fe PA, *56*	110	270	_____
474/475	Rocket PA/PA, *53–55*			
	(A) Chromed, *53*	125	380	_____
	(B) Silver-painted, *54–55*	105	335	_____
476	Rocket PB, *55**		NRS	_____
477/478	Silver Flash PA/PB, *53–54*			
	(A) Chromed, *53*	170	510	_____
	(B) Silver-painted, *54*	160	485	_____
479	Silver Flash PA, *55*	80	270	_____
480	Silver Flash PB, *55**	—	1150	_____
481	Silver Flash PA, *56*	110	315	_____
484/485/486	Santa Fe PA/PB/PA, *56–57*	225	670	_____
490/491/493	Northern Pacific PA/PB/PA, *56**	435	1650	_____
490/492	Northern Pacific PA/PA, *57*	215	740	_____

		Good	Exc	Cond/$
494/495	New Haven PA/PA, *56*	220	810	_____
497	New Haven PA, *57*	110	360	_____
499	New Haven GE Electric, *56–57*	130	475	_____
500	AFL Combination Car, *52 u*			
	(A) Silver finish	135	510	_____
	(B) Chrome finish	110	380	_____
501	AFL Passenger Car, *52 u*			
	(A) Silver finish	150	530	_____
	(B) Chrome finish	125	415	_____
502	AFL Vista Dome Car, *52 u*			
	(A) Silver finish	145	510	_____
	(B) Chrome finish	125	415	_____
503	AFL Observation Car, *52 u*	145	510	_____
520	Knuckle Coupler Kit, *54–56*	2	5	_____
521	Knuckle Coupler Kit		NRS	_____
525	Knuckle Coupler Trucks		NRS	_____
526	Knuckle Coupler Trucks		NRS	_____
529	Knuckle Coupler Trucks		NRS	_____
530	Knuckle Coupler Trucks		NRS	_____
532	Knuckle Coupler Trucks		NRS	_____
541	Fuses, *46*		NRS	_____
561	Billboard Horn, *55–56*	20	50	_____
566	Whistling Billboard, *51–55*	15	46	_____
568	Whistling Billboard, *56*	18	41	_____
571	Truss Bridge, *55–56*	11	37	_____
573	American Flyer Talking Station Record		NRS	_____
577	Whistling Billboard, *46–50*			
	(A) Circus, *46–47*	22	65	_____
	(B) Fox Mart, *47*	—	1650	_____
	(C) Trains, *50*	23	44	_____
578	Station Figure set, *46–52*	50	155	_____
579	Single Street Lamp, *46–49*	10	50	_____
580	Double Street Lamp, *46–49*	12	50	_____
581	Girder Bridge, *46–56*	11	33	_____
582	Blinker Signal, *46–48*	47	125	_____
583	Electromagnetic Crane, *46–49*	50	160	_____
583A	Electromagnetic Crane, *50–53*	55	155	_____
584	Bell Danger Signal, *46–47*	190	720	_____
585	Tool Shed, *46–52*	22	55	_____
586F	Wayside Station, *46–56*	27	95	_____
587	Block Signal, *46–47*	65	220	_____

		Good	Exc	Cond/$
588	Semaphore Block Signal, *46–48*	660	1750	_____
589	Passenger and Freight Station, *46–56*			
	(A) Green-painted roof	15	60	_____
	(B) Black-painted roof	15	75	_____
590	Control Tower, *55–56*	24	75	_____
591	Crossing Gate, *46–48*	20	75	_____
592	Crossing Gate, *49–50*	22	70	_____
592A	Crossing Gate, *51–53*	22	70	_____
593	Signal Tower, *46–54*	40	85	_____
594	Animated Track Gang, *46–47**	590	2350	_____
596	Operating Water Tank, *46–56*	39	85	_____
598	Talking Station Record, *46–56*	11	24	_____
599	Talking Station Record, *56*	12	39	_____
600	Crossing Gate w/ bell, *54–56*	29	85	_____
605	American Flyer Lines Flatcar, *53*	10	37	_____
606	American Flyer Lines Crane, *53*	15	46	_____
607	AFL Work and Boom Car, *53*	10	36	_____
609	American Flyer Lines Flatcar, *53*	10	37	_____
612	Freight Passenger Station w/ Crane, *46–51, 53–54*	48	95	_____
613	Great Northern Boxcar, *53*	19	60	_____
620	Southern Gondola, *53*	21	75	_____
621	½ Straight Track, *46–48*	0.20	0.55	_____
622	½ Curved Track, *46–48*	0.20	0.55	_____
622	GAEX Boxcar, *53**	16	70	_____
623	Illinois Central Reefer, *53**	11	32	_____
625	Shell Tank Car, *46–50*			
	(A) Orange tanks	345	690	_____
	(B) Black tanks	11	37	_____
	(C) Silver tanks	5	26	_____
625	Gulf Tank Car, *51*	9	23	_____
625G	Gulf Tank Car, *51–53 u*	9	23	_____
627	C&NWRY Flatcar (mv), *46–50*	10	26	_____
627	American Flyer Lines Flatcar, *50*	11	34	_____
(628)	C&NWRY Flatcar, *46–53*			
	(A) Metal	9	32	_____
	(B) Wood	13	47	_____
629	Missouri Pacific Stock Car (mv), *46–53*	10	26	_____
630	Reading Caboose (mv), *46–53*	5	17	_____
630	American Flyer Caboose, *53*	10	41	_____
630	American Flyer Lines Caboose, *52 u*	9	28	_____

		Good	Exc	Cond/$
631	Texas & Pacific Gondola, *46–53*			
	(A) Green unpainted	8	15	_____
	(B) Dark gray unpainted, *48 u*	70	270	_____
	(C) Red-painted, *52 u*	27	120	_____
	(D) Green-painted, *46–52*	5	18	_____
(632)	Virginian Hopper, *46*	32	105	_____
632	Lehigh New England Hopper, *46–53*			
	(A) Gray-painted, die-cast, *46*	31	115	_____
	(B) Black plastic, *46*	8	21	_____
	(C) Gray plastic	5	18	_____
	(D) White plastic	30	115	_____
	(E) Painted body	8	20	_____
633	Baltimore & Ohio Boxcars (mv), *46–52*	10	25	_____
633	Baltimore & Ohio Reefers (mv), *46–52*			
	(A) Red, *52 u*	35	120	_____
	(B) Tuscan, *52 u*	40	125	_____
633F	G. Fox & Co. Boxcar, *47 u**	1050	2700	_____
634	C&NWRY Floodlight (mv), *46–49, 53*	11	43	_____
635	C&NWRY Crane, *46–48*	15	60	_____
(635)	C&NWRY Crane, *48–49*			
	(A) Yellow cab	12	48	_____
	(B) Red cab	80	270	_____
	(C) Black roof		NRS	_____
636	Erie Flatcar, *48–53*			
	(A) Die-cast metal frame	14	40	_____
	(B) Pressed-wood frame, *53 u*	75	320	_____
637	MKT Boxcar (mv), *49–53**	7	28	_____
638	American Flyer Caboose (mv), *50–52*	4	10	_____
638	American Flyer Lines Caboose, *53*	4	11	_____
639	American Flyer Boxcars (mv), *49–52*			
	(A) Yellow body	6	18	_____
	(B) Tuscan body	15	65	_____
639	American Flyer Reefers (mv), *49–52*			
	(A) Yellow body	6	18	_____
	(B) Unpainted cream plastic body	40	150	_____
640	American Flyer Hopper, *49–53*			
	(A) White lettering	4	14	_____
	(B) Black lettering	5	16	_____
	(C) White plastic body w/ black lettering	14	55	_____
640	Wabash Hopper, *53*	9	34	_____

		Good	Exc	Cond/$
641	American Flyer Gondola, *49–52*			
	(A) Red-painted or unpainted plastic	11	25	_____
	(B) Gray unpainted, *51 u*	50	230	_____
641	Frisco Gondola, *53*	11	28	_____
642	American Flyer Boxcars, *51–52*	9	17	_____
642	American Flyer Reefers, *52 u*	8	25	_____
642	Seaboard Boxcar, *53*	9	27	_____
(643)	American Flyer Circus Flatcar, *50–53**			
	(A) Yellow, metal	80	255	_____
	(B) Yellow, wood	100	395	_____
	(C) Red, metal	120	450	_____
644	American Flyer Crane, *50–53*			
	(A) Red cab, black boom, *50*	39	130	_____
	(B) Red cab, green boom, *50*	20	70	_____
	(C) Tuscan-painted cab, green boom, *50–51*	25	80	_____
	(D) Black cab, boom	20	70	_____
645	AF Work and Boom Car, *50*	16	37	_____
645A	AFL Work and Boom Car, *51–53*	15	36	_____
(646)	Erie Floodlight, *50–53*			
	(A) Green-painted die-cast generator, *50*	49	220	_____
	(B) Other variations	16	42	_____
647	Northern Pacific Reefer, *52–53*	13	48	_____
648	American Flyer Flatcar, *52–54*	11	39	_____
(649)	AF Circus Passenger Car (mv), *50–52*	46	115	_____
650	New Haven Pullman Car (mv), *46–53*			
	(A) Red or green w/ plastic frame	21	75	_____
	(B) Red or green w/ die-cast frame	22	65	_____
	(C) Red or green w/ sheet metal frame	18	55	_____
651	New Haven Baggage Car (mv), *46–53*			
	(A) Red or green w/ plastic frame	12	55	_____
	(B) Red or green w/ die-cast frame	12	55	_____
	(C) Red or green w/ sheet metal frame	12	55	_____
652	Pullman (mv), *46–53*			
	(A) Red, tuscan, or green, short trucks	46	145	_____
	(B) Red or green, long trucks	65	220	_____
	(C) Red, tuscan, or green, "Pikes Peak"	50	165	_____
653	Pullman (mv), *46–53*			
	(A) Red or green, long trucks	65	220	_____
	(B) Red, tuscan, or green, short trucks	44	140	_____

		Good	Exc	Cond/$
654	Pullman Observation Car (mv), *46–53*			
	(A) Red or green, long trucks	65	220	_____
	(B) Red, tuscan, or green, short trucks	42	130	_____
655	Silver Bullet Passenger Car, *53*			
	(A) Chrome	25	100	_____
	(B) Satin aluminum	20	85	_____
655	AFL Passenger Car, *53*			
	(A) Tuscan	22	70	_____
	(B) Green	22	70	_____
660	AFL Combination Car, *50–52*			
	(A) Extruded aluminum shell	20	65	_____
	(B) Chrome-finished, plastic shell	30	95	_____
	(C) Satin silver			
661	AFL Passenger Car, *50–52*			
	(A) Extruded aluminum shell	34	75	_____
	(B) Chrome-finished, plastic shell	45	95	_____
	(C) Satin silver			
662	AFL Vista Dome Car, *50–52*			
	(A) Extruded aluminum shell	22	70	_____
	(B) Chrome-finished, plastic shell	30	95	_____
663	AFL Observation Car, *50–52*	25	80	_____
668	Manual Switch, LH, *53–55*	5	10	_____
669	Manual Switch, RH, *53–55*	5	10	_____
670	Track Trip, *55–56*	2	17	_____
678	RC Switch, LH, *53–56*	7	16	_____
679	RC Switch, RH, *53–56*	7	16	_____
680	Curved Track, *46–48*	0.20	0.50	_____
681	Straight Track, *46–48*	0.25	0.55	_____
688	RC Switches, pair, *46–48*	20	50	_____
690	Track Terminal, *46–56*	0.50	1	_____
691	Steel Pins, *46–48*	0.50	1	_____
692	Fiber Pins, *46–48*	0.30	0.85	_____
693	Track Locks, *48–56*	0.05	0.15	_____
694	Coupler, Truck, Wheels, Axles, *46–53*	3	10	_____
695	Track Trip, *46*	14	14	_____
695	Reverse Loop Relay, *55–56*	27	75	_____
696	Track Trip, *55–57*			
	(A) Plastic shoe	10	20	_____
	(B) Die-cast shoe	10	29	_____
697	Track Trip, *50–54*	4	10	_____
698	Reverse Loop Kit, *49–50, 52–54*	16	49	_____
700	Straight Track, *46–56*	0.50	1	_____

		Good	Exc	Cond/$
701	½ Straight Track, *46–56*	0.25	0.75	_____
702	Curved Track, *46–56*	0.15	0.40	_____
703	½ Curved Track, *46–56*	0.10	0.20	_____
704	Manual Uncoupler, *52–56*	0.30	0.55	_____
705	RC Uncoupler, *46–47*	1	4	_____
706	RC Uncoupler, *48–56*	0.50	2	_____
707	Track Terminal, *46–59*	0.15	0.90	_____
708	Air Chime Whistle Control, *51–56*	3	10	_____
709	Lockout Eliminator, *50–55*	2	8	_____
710	Steam Whistle Control, *55–56*	8	34	_____
710	Automatic Track Section, *46–47*	0.50	1.50	_____
711	Mail Pickup, *46–47*	9	21	_____
712	Special Rail Section, *47–56*	0.50	1	_____
713	Special Rail Section w/ mail bag hook, *47–56*	8	21	_____
714	Log Unloading Car Flatcar, *51–54*	15	60	_____
715	American Flyer Lines Flatcar (mv), *46–54*			
	(A) Armored car	21	85	_____
	(B) Racer	19	70	_____
716	American Flyer Lines Hopper, *46–51*			
	(A) 46	7	31	_____
	(B) 47–51	6	22	_____
717	American Flyer Lines Flatcar, *46–52*	12	50	_____
718	New Haven Mail Pickup (mv), *46–54*			
	(A) Red or green	32	85	_____
	(B) Red pickup arm	175	440	_____
	(C) Tuscan		NRS	_____
719	CB&Q Hopper Dump Car, *50–54*			
	(A) Tuscan-painted	25	80	_____
	(B) Red plastic	30	100	_____
720	RC Switches, *46–49*	19	48	_____
720A	RC Switches, *50–56*	25	50	_____
722	Manual Switches, *46–51*	10	20	_____
722A	Manual Switches, *52–56*	10	20	_____
725	Crossing, *46–56*	2	5	_____
726	Straight Rubber Roadbed, *50–56*	0.50	2	_____
727	Curved Rubber Roadbed, *50–56*	0.50	2	_____
728	Re-railer, *56*	2	10	_____
730	Bumper, *46–56*			
	(A) Green plastic	10	18	_____
	(B) Red, *51*	31	110	_____
	(C) Green painted	26	95	_____

		Good	Exc	Cond/$
731	Pike Planning Kit, *52–56*	10	27	_____
732	AF Operating Baggage Car, *51–54*			
	(A) Unpainted red or green plastic body	32	85	_____
	(B) Green-painted plastic body	40	100	_____
734	American Flyer Operating Boxcar, *50–54*	24	70	_____
735	NH Animated Station Coach, *52–54*	30	85	_____
736	Missouri Pacific Stock Car, *50–54*	10	31	_____
(740)	American Flyer Lines Motorized Handcar			
	(A) No decals, no vent holes, *52*	30	90	_____
	(B) w/ shield decal	15	65	_____
741	AFL Handcar and Shed, motorized unit, *53*	80	210	_____
(742)	AFL Motorized Handcar, *55–56*	39	140	_____
743	See (23)743			
747	Cardboard Trestle set, u	7	24	_____
748	Overhead Foot Bridge, *51–52*			
	(A) Gray/aluminum	10	30	_____
	(B) Bluish-silver	30	50	_____
748	Girder, Trestle, Tower Bridge, *58 u*	21	42	_____
749	Street Lamp set, *50–52*	6	22	_____
750	Trestle Bridge, *46–56*	14	50	_____
751	Log Loader, *46–50*	36	145	_____
751A	Log Loader, *52–53*	41	160	_____
752	Seaboard Coaler, *46–50*	85	230	_____
752A	Seaboard Coaler, *51–52*	115	260	_____
753	Single Trestle Bridge, *52*	15	60	_____
753	Mountain, Tunnel, Pass set, *60 u*	19	43	_____
754	Double Trestle Bridge, *50–52*	38	85	_____
755	Talking Station, *48–50*			
	(A) Green roof	50	100	_____
	(B) Blue roof	85	140	_____
758	Sam the Semaphore Man, *49*	28	90	_____
758A	Sam the Semaphore Man, *50–56*	35	95	_____
759	Bell Danger Signal (mv), *53–56*	20	70	_____
760	Highway Flasher, *49–56*	10	41	_____
761	Semaphore, *49–56*	22	70	_____
762	Two in One Whistle, *49–50*	37	90	_____
763	Mountain set, *49–50*	45	180	_____
764	Express Office, *50–51*	45	150	_____
766	Animated Station, *52–54*	41	145	_____
K766	Animated Station, *53–55*	50	195	_____
767	Roadside Diner, *50–54*	40	100	_____

		Good	Exc	Cond/$
768	Oil Supply Depot, *50–53*			
	(A) "Shell"	40	110	_____
	(B) "Gulf"	50	140	_____
769	Aircraft Beacon, *50*	15	50	_____
769A	Aircraft Beacon, *51–56*	15	50	_____
770	Loading Platform, *50–52*	32	85	_____
770	Girder Trestle set, *60 u*	5	18	_____
771	Operating Stockyard, *50–54*	40	110	_____
K771	Stockyard and Car, *53–56*	42	125	_____
772	Water Tower, *50–56*			
	(A) Small tank	30	90	_____
	(B) Checkerboard, metal shack	37	115	_____
	(C) Checkerboard, plastic shack	55	145	_____
773	Oil Derrick, *50–52*			
	(A) "American Flyer", *50*	44	130	_____
	(B) "Gulf" logo		NRS	_____
774	Floodlight Tower (mv), *51–56*	16	65	_____
775	Baggage Platform w/ LC Car, *53–55*	21	75	_____
K775	Baggage Platform w/ KC Car, *53–55*	32	95	_____
778	Street Lamp set, *53–56*	12	35	_____
779	Oil Drum Loader, *55–56*	49	135	_____
780	Trestle set, *53–56*	6	18	_____
781	Abutment set, *53*	20	50	_____
782	Abutment set, *53*	15	46	_____
783	Hi-Trestle Sections, *53–56*	5	19	_____
784	Hump set, *55*	65	220	_____
785	Coal Loader, *55–56*	115	285	_____
787	Log Loader, *55–56*	70	255	_____
788	Suburban Station, *56*	10	47	_____
789	Station and Baggage Smasher, *56–57*	55	195	_____
790	Trainorama, *53 u*	50	130	_____
792	Terminal, *54–56*	70	215	_____
793	Union Station, *55–56*	15	110	_____
794	Union Station, *54*	30	125	_____
795	Union Station and Terminal, *54*	95	465	_____
799	Talking Station, *54–56*	31	170	_____
801	Baltimore & Ohio Hopper, *56–57*	12	23	_____
802	Illinois Central Reefer, *56–57**	11	21	_____
803	Santa Fe Boxcar, *56–57*	18	30	_____
804	Norfolk & Western Gondola, *56–57*	8	15	_____
805	Pennsylvania Gondola, *56–57*	8	15	_____
806	American Flyer Lines Caboose, *56–57*	9	11	_____

		Good	Exc	Cond/$
807	Rio Grande Boxcar, *57*			
	(A) Non-opening door	17	31	_____
	(B) Opening door		NRS	_____
812	See (21)812			
900	NP Combination Car, *56–57**	110	320	_____
901	NP Passenger Car, *56–57**	110	320	_____
902	NP Vista Dome Car, *56–57**	110	320	_____
903	NP Observation Car, *56–57**	110	320	_____
904	American Flyer Lines Caboose, *56*	10	19	_____
905	American Flyer Lines Flatcar, *54*	11	44	_____
906	American Flyer Lines Crane, *54*	16	47	_____
907	AFL Work and Boom Car, *54*	11	43	_____
909	American Flyer Lines Flatcar, *54*	11	43	_____
910	Gilbert Chemical Tank Car, *54**	80	270	_____
911	C&O Gondola, *55–57*			
	(A) Silver pipes	10	36	_____
	(B) Brown plastic pipes	30	110	_____
912	Koppers Tank Car, *55–56*	17	80	_____
913	Great Northern Boxcar, *53–58*			
	(A) Decal	15	41	_____
	(B) Stamped	16	42	_____
914	American Flyer Lines Flatcar, *53–57*	17	65	_____
915	American Flyer Lines Flatcar (mv), *53–57*	16	75	_____
916	Delaware & Hudson Gondola, *55–56*	8	31	_____
918	American Flyer Lines Mail Car, *53–58*			
	(A) "American Flyer Lines"	30	95	_____
	(B) "New Haven"	35	110	_____
919	CB&Q Hopper Dump Car, *53–56*	22	95	_____
920	Southern Gondola, *53–56*	9	27	_____
921	CB&Q Hopper, *53–56*	8	31	_____
922	GAEX Boxcar, *53–57**			
	(A) Decal	15	41	_____
	(B) Stamped	15	41	_____
923	Illinois Central Reefer, *54–55**	12	23	_____
924	CRP Hopper, *53–56*	8	27	_____
925	Gulf Tank Car, *52–56*	12	23	_____
926	Gulf Tank Car, *55–56*	12	55	_____
(928)	C&NWRY Flatcar, *53–54*			
	(A) Pressed-wood base	22	70	_____
	(B) Die-cast base	10	26	_____
928	New Haven Flatcar (Log Car), *54*	10	37	_____
928	New Haven Flatcar (Lumber Car), *56–57*	11	37	_____

		Good	Exc	Cond/$
929	Missouri Pacific Stock Car, *53–56*	11	32	_____
930	American Flyer Caboose, *52*			
	(A) Early knuckle coupler	25	70	_____
	(B) Red	15	50	_____
	(C) Tuscan	10	31	_____
930	American Flyer Lines Caboose, *53–57*			
	(A) Type I or II body	10	31	_____
	(B) Type III body	35	110	_____
931	Texas & Pacific Gondola, *53–55*	5	16	_____
933	B&O Boxcar, *53–54*	15	40	_____
934	American Flyer Lines Caboose, u	17	65	_____
934	C&NWRY Floodlight, *53–54*	9	33	_____
934	Southern Pacific Floodlight, *54 u*	13	49	_____
935	AFL Bay Window Caboose, *57*	21	90	_____
936	Erie Flatcar, *53–56*	12	40	_____
936	Pennsylvania Flatcar, *53–57*	40	145	_____
937	MKT Boxcar, *53–58**			
	(A) All yellow	10	41	_____
	(B) Yellow and brown	10	41	_____
938	American Flyer Lines Caboose, *54–55*	4	13	_____
940	Wabash Hopper, *53–56*	5	22	_____
941	Frisco Lines Gondola, *53–56*	6	17	_____
942	Seaboard Boxcar, *54*	10	31	_____
944	American Flyer Crane, *52–56*	22	65	_____
945	AFL Work and Boom Car, *53–57*	12	46	_____
(946)	Erie Floodlight (mv), *53–56*	10	41	_____
947	Northern Pacific Reefer, *53–58*	12	44	_____
948	AFL Flatcar, *53–56*	10	34	_____
951	AFL Baggage Car (mv), *53–57*			
	(A) Red or tuscan	15	50	_____
	(B) Green	20	60	_____
952	AFL Pullman Car, *53–58*			
	(A) w/o silhouettes, tuscan or green	36	155	_____
	(B) w/ silhouettes, tuscan	55	225	_____
953	AFL Combination Car, *53–58*			
	(A) w/o silhouettes, tuscan or green	36	155	_____
	(B) w/ silhouettes, tuscan	55	220	_____
954	AFL Observation Car, *53–56*			
	(A) w/o silhouettes, tuscan or green	36	155	_____
	(B) w/ silhouettes, tuscan	105	220	_____

		Good	Exc	Cond/$
955	AFL Passenger Car, *54*			
	(A) Satin silver-painted	30	100	_____
	(B) Green-painted	35	120	_____
	(C) Tuscan-painted w/ silhouettes and "955"	20	85	_____
	(D) Tuscan-painted w/ silhouettes and white-outlined windows	31	115	_____
956	Monon Flatcar, *56*	20	80	_____
957	Erie Operating Boxcar, *57 u*	44	150	_____
958	Mobilgas Tank Car, *57 u*	21	85	_____
960	AFL Columbus Combination Car, *53–56*			
	(A) No color band	30	115	_____
	(B) Blue, green, or red band	42	130	_____
	(C) Chestnut band	75	250	_____
	(D) Orange band	55	190	_____
961	AFL Jefferson Pullman Car, *53–58*			
	(A) No color band	40	130	_____
	(B) Blue band			
	(C) Green or red band	40	130	_____
	(D) Chestnut band	105	340	_____
	(E) Orange band	70	215	_____
962	AFL Hamilton Vista Dome Car, *53–58*			
	(A) No color band	40	140	_____
	(B) Blue, green, or red band	41	145	_____
	(C) Chestnut band	95	315	_____
	(D) Orange band	70	205	_____
963	AFL Washington Passenger Car, *53–58*			
	(A) No color band	41	145	_____
	(B) Blue, green, or red band	40	140	_____
	(C) Chestnut band	95	335	_____
	(D) Orange band	70	210	_____
969	Rocket Launcher Flatcar, *57 u*	21	75	_____
970	Seaboard Operating Boxcar, *56–57*	27	70	_____
971	Southern Pacific Flatcar, *56–57*	36	140	_____
973	Gilbert's Operating Milk Car, *56–57*	55	150	_____
974	AFL Operating Boxcar, *53–54*	27	75	_____
974	Erie Operating Boxcar, *55*	45	135	_____
975	AFL Operating Coach, *55*	32	95	_____
976	MoPac Operating Cattle Car, *53–62*	22	60	_____
977	American Flyer Lines Caboose, *55–57*	22	55	_____
978	AFL Grand Canyon Obsv. Car, *56–58*	130	420	_____
979	AFL bay window Caboose, *57*	36	125	_____
980	Baltimore & Ohio Boxcar, *56–57*	31	125	_____

		Good	Exc	Cond/$
981	Central of Georgia Boxcar, *56*			
	(A) Shiny black paint	43	130	_____
	(B) Dull black paint	50	145	_____
982	BAR Boxcar, *56–57*	42	125	_____
983	MoPac Boxcar, *56–57*	45	135	_____
984	New Haven Boxcar, *56–57*	25	95	_____
985	BM Boxcar, *57*	50	125	_____
988	ART Co. Reefer, *56*	37	115	_____
989	Northwestern Reefer, *56–58*	41	155	_____
994	Union Pacific Stock Car, *57*	55	185	_____
C1001	WSX Boxcar, *62 u**	365	1250	_____
C2001	Post Boxcar, *62 u*	10	31	_____
L2001	Game Train 4-4-0, *63*	16	38	_____
L2002	Burlington Route 4-4-0, *63 u*	55	240	_____
L-2004	Rio Grande EMD F-9, *62*	80	210	_____
C-2009	Texas & Pacific Gondola, *62–64*			
	(A) Dark green		NRS	_____
	(B) Light green	5	16	_____
7210	See (636), (646), 936, (946), or (24529)			
1-1024 A	Trestle set, *52 u*	10	45	_____
21004	PRR 0-6-0 Switcher, *57 u*	105	360	_____
21005	PRR 0-6-0 Switcher, *57–58*	130	460	_____
(21030)	See 307			
(21034)	See 303			
(21044)	See 313			
(21058)	See 326			
21084	CNW 4-6-2, Pacific, *57 u*	40	135	_____
21085	CNW or CMStP&P 4-6-2 Pacific, *58–65*	35	100	_____
(210)88	FY&P 4-4-0 Franklin, *59–60*	42	120	_____
(21089)	FY&PRR 4-4-0 Wash., *60–61*	70	275	_____
21095	NYNH&H 4-6-2 Pacific, *57*		NRS	_____
21099	NYNH&H 4-6-2 Pacific, *58*	100	305	_____
21100	Reading 4-4-2 Atlantic, *57 u*	15	41	_____
21105	Reading 4-4-2 Atlantic, *57–58*	15	41	_____
21106	Reading 4-4-2 Atlantic, *59 u*	60	180	_____
21107	PRR or BN 4-4-2 Atlantic, *64–65 u*	10	36	_____
21115	PRR 4-6-2 Pacific, *58*	225	890	_____
21129	NYC 4-6-4 Hudson, *58*	275	1200	_____
21130	NYC 4-6-4 Hudson, *59–60*	130	370	_____
21139	UP 4-8-4 Northern, *58–59*	215	790	_____
21140	UP 4-8-4 Northern, *60*	400	1600	_____
21145	NKP 0-8-0 Switcher, *58*	175	640	_____

		Good	Exc	Cond/$
21155	Steam 0-6-0 Switcher, *58*	85	305	_____
21156	Steam 0-6-0 Switcher, *59*	70	255	_____
21158	Steam 0-6-0 Switcher, *60 u*	40	135	_____
21160	Reading 4-4-2 Atlantic, *58–60 u*	13	33	_____
21161	Reading 4-4-2 Atlantic, *60 u*			
	(A) "American Flyer Lines"	11	27	_____
	(B) "Prestone Car Care Express"	65	240	_____
21165	Erie 4-4-0, *61–62, 65–66 u*	10	25	_____
21166	Burlington Route 4-4-0, *63–64, 65–66 u*			
	(A) White letters	10	25	_____
	(B) Black letters	75	225	_____
21168	Southern 4-4-0, *61–63*	29	80	_____
21205/21205-1	BM twin EMD F-9s, *61, 62 u*			
	(A) Twin A units (u)	110	280	_____
	(B) Single unit	80	200	_____
21206/21206-1	SF twin EMD F-9s, *62 u*	100	240	_____
21207/21207-1	GN twin EMD F-9s, *63–64*	100	310	_____
21210	Burlington EMD F-9, *61*	60	185	_____
21215/21215-1	UP EMD F-9, *61–62*	90	250	_____
21215/21216	UP twin EMD F-9s, *61*		NRS	_____
(21)234	Chesapeake & Ohio GP-7, *60–61*			
	(A) Long steps	150	530	_____
	(B) Short steps	180	640	_____
21551	Northern Pacific PA, *58*			
	(A) Plastic steps	140	365	_____
	(B) Sheet-metal steps	160	435	_____
(21552/21556)	See 490/492			
(21560)	See 497			
21561	New Haven PA, *57–58*			
	(A) Plastic steps	130	355	_____
	(B) One-rivet metal steps	150	400	_____
(21570)	See 499			
(21571)	See 499			
21573	New Haven GE Electric, *58–59*	155	530	_____
21720	Santa Fe PB, *58 u*	360	1350	_____
(21800)	See 355			
21801	CNW Baldwin, *57–58*			
	(A) Unpainted	50	190	_____
	(B) Painted	70	220	_____
21801-1	CNW Baldwin, *58 u*			
	(A) Unpainted	75	230	_____
	(B) Painted	90	260	_____

		Good	Exc	Cond/$
21808	CNW Baldwin, *58 u*	50	140	_____
(21)812	Texas & Pacific Baldwin, *59–60*	70	200	_____
21813	M&StL Baldwin, *58 u*	205	610	_____
(21820)	See 372			
(21821)	See 372			
21831	Texas & Pacific GP-7, *58*			
	(A) "American Flyer Lines"	155	445	_____
	(B) "Texas & Pacific"	195	580	_____
21910/21910-1/21910-2	SF PA/PB/PA, *57–58*	325	900	_____
21918/21918-1	Seaboard Baldwin, *58*	340	830	_____
21920/21920-1	MP, PA/PA, *58**	380	1300	_____
21920	MP, PA, *63–64*	160	630	_____
21922/21922-1	MP, PA/PA, *59*	300	1000	_____
21925/21925-1	UP, PA/PA, *59–60**	290	1150	_____
21927	Santa Fe PA, *60–62*	140	320	_____
22004	40-watt Transformer, *59–64*	2	9	_____
22006	25-watt Transformer, *63*	2	10	_____
22020	50-watt Transformer, *57–64*	2	6	_____
22030	100-watt Transformer, *57–64*	5	16	_____
22033	25-watt Transformer, *65*	2	5	_____
22034	110-watt Transformer, *65*	5	16	_____
22035	175-watt Transformer, *57–64*	16	60	_____
22040	110-watt Transformer, *57–58*	6	20	_____
22050	175-watt Transformer, *57–58*	13	37	_____
22060	175-watt Transformer, *57–58*	13	37	_____
22080	300-watt Transformer, *57–58*	32	105	_____
22090	350-watt Transformer, *59–64*	41	135	_____
23021	Imitation Grass, *57–59*	5	21	_____
23022	Scenery Gravel, *57–59*	5	21	_____
23023	Imitation Coal, *57–59*	4	12	_____
23024	Rainbow Wire, *57–64*	4	11	_____
23025	Smoke Cartridges, *57–59*	4	11	_____
23026	Service Kit, *59–64*	5	21	_____
23027	Track Cleaning Fluid, *57–59*	2	5	_____
23028	Smoke Fluid Dispenser, *60–64*	2	5	_____
23032	Equipment Kit, *60–61*	37	105	_____
23036	Money Saver Kit, *60, 62, 64*	35	100	_____
23040	Mountain, Tunnel, and Pass set, *58*		NRS	_____
23249	Tunnel, *57–64*	10	41	_____
23320	AF Traffic Master, *60*		NM	_____
23561	Billboard Horn, *57–59*	10	41	_____
23568	Whistling Billboard, *57–64*	10	50	_____

		Good	Exc	Cond/$
23571	Truss Bridge, *57–64*	5	19	_____
23581	Girder Bridge, *57–64*	8	31	_____
23586	Wayside Station, *57–59*	25	90	_____
23589	Passenger and Freight Station, *59 u*	15	50	_____
23590	Control Tower, *57–59*	20	70	_____
23596	Water Tank, *57–58*	26	90	_____
23598	Talking Station Record, *57–59*	5	21	_____
23599	Talking Station Record, *57*	10	40	_____
23600	Crossing Gate w/ bell, *57–58*	13	70	_____
23601	Crossing Gate, *59–62*	11	44	_____
23602	Crossing Gate, *63–64*	11	44	_____
(23)743	Track Maintenance Car		—	_____
23743	Track Maintenance Car, *60–64*	100	200	_____
23750	Trestle Bridge, *57–61*	22	60	_____
23758	Sam the Semaphore Man, *57*	27	80	_____
23759	Bell Danger Signal, *56–60*	12	50	_____
23760	Highway Flasher, *57–60*	10	41	_____
23761	Semaphore, *57–60*	18	46	_____
23763	Bell Danger Signal, *61–64*	11	43	_____
23764	Flasher Signal, *61–64*	11	29	_____
23769	Aircraft Beacon, *57–64*	12	55	_____
23771	Stockyard and Car, *57–61*	32	105	_____
23772	Water Tower, *57–64*	21	105	_____
23774	Floodlight Tower, *57–64*	16	47	_____
23778	Street Lamp set, *57–64*	8	30	_____
23779	Oil Drum Loader, *57–61*	47	135	_____
23780	Gabe the Lamplighter, *58–59*			
	(A) Plastic shed		NRS	_____
	(B) Metal shed	305	910	_____
23785	Coal Loader, *57–60*	130	320	_____
23786	Talking Station, *57–59*	55	120	_____
23787	Log Loader, *57–60*	75	250	_____
23788	Suburban Station, *57–64*	10	41	_____
23789	Station and Baggage Smasher, *58–59*	55	185	_____
23791	Cow-on-Track, *57–59*	23	85	_____
23796	Sawmill, *57–64*	90	255	_____
23830	Piggyback Unloader, *59–60*	32	105	_____
24003	Santa Fe Boxcar, *58*			
	(A) Unpainted	15	46	_____
	(B) Painted		—	_____
24006	Great Northern Boxcar, *57*		NRS	_____
24016	MKT Boxcar, *58*	215	850	_____

		Good	Exc	Cond/$
24019	Seaboard Boxcar, *58 u*	15	42	_____
(24022)	See 980			
24023	Baltimore & Ohio Boxcar, *58–59*	35	165	_____
(24025)	See 981			
24026	Central of Georgia Boxcar, *58*	30	150	_____
24029	BAR Boxcar, *57–60*	36	145	_____
24030	MKT Boxcar, *60 u*			
	(A) Unpainted yellow plastic	10	26	_____
	(B) Yellow-painted plastic			
24033	Missouri Pacific Boxcar, *58*	49	130	_____
24035	See 984			
24036	New Haven Boxcar, *58*	30	95	_____
24039	Rio Grande Boxcar, *59*	10	47	_____
24042	See 985			
24043	Boston & Maine Boxcar, *58–60*	32	105	_____
24045	MEC Boxcar		NRS	_____
24047	Great Northern Boxcar, *59*	50	225	_____
24048	M&StL Boxcar, *59–62*	42	115	_____
24052	UFGE Boxcar, *61*	11	22	_____
24054	Santa Fe Boxcar, *62–64, 66*			
	(A) Red-painted plastic, *62–64*	20	50	_____
	(B) Red unpainted plastic, *66*	10	50	_____
(240)55	The Gold Belt Line Boxcar, *60–61*			
	(A) Opening w/ door	15	50	_____
	(B) Opening w/o door	15	50	_____
24056	Boston & Maine Boxcar, *61*			
	(A) Blue-painted black plastic	55	180	_____
	(B) Unpainted blue plastic	25	120	_____
24057	Mounds Boxcar, *62*			
	(A) White	6	21	_____
	(B) Ivory	10	26	_____
24058	Post Boxcar, *63–64*			
	(A) "Cereal"	8	18	_____
	(B) "Cereals"	11	24	_____
24059	Boston & Maine Boxcar, *63*	50	175	_____
24060	M&StL Boxcar, *63–64*	40	140	_____
24065	NYC Boxcar, *60–64*			
	(A) Knuckle couplers	39	105	_____
	(B) Pike Master couplers	30	80	_____
24066	L&N Boxcar, *60*			
	(A) Black plastic body	75	170	_____
	(B) White plastic body	90	185	_____

		Good	Exc	Cond/$
(24067)	Keystone Line Boxcar, *60 u**	1050	1650	_____
24068	Planters Peanuts Boxcar, *61 u**		NRS	_____
(24072)	See 929			
(24075)	See 994			
24076	Union Pacific Stock Car (mv), *57–60*			
	(A) w/ knuckle couplers	24	70	_____
	(B) w/ Pike Master couplers	20	60	_____
24077	Northern Pacific Stock Car, *59–62*			
	(A) Knuckle couplers	85	235	_____
	(B) Pike Master couplers	60	200	_____
24103	Norfolk & Western Gondola, *58, 63–64*			
	(A) Black plastic	6	18	_____
	(B) Brown plastic		NRS	_____
24106	Pennsylvania Gondola, *60 u*			
	(A) Unpainted	5	13	_____
	(B) Painted	20	70	_____
(24108)	See 911			
24109	C&O Gondola, *57–60*			
	(A) Silver plastic or cardboard pipes	18	55	_____
	(B) Brown plastic pipes	35	120	_____
	(C) Orange cardboard pipes	20	60	_____
24110	Pennsylvania Gondola, *59 u*	5	15	_____
(24112)	See 916			
24113	Delaware & Hudson Gondola, *57–59*	11	42	_____
(24115)	See 920			
24116	Southern Gondola, *57–60*	12	55	_____
24120	Texas & Pacific Gondola, *60*	12	55	_____
(24122)	See 941			
24124	Boston & Maine Gondola, *63–64*			
	(A) Unpainted blue	5	21	_____
	(B) Dark blue-painted	28	105	_____
24125	Bethlehem Steel Gondola, *60–64*			
	(A) Gray-painted	6	17	_____
	(B) Unpainted gray	29	95	_____
24126	Frisco Gondola, *61*	37	130	_____
24127	Monon Gondola, *61–65*			
	(A) Knuckle couplers	5	15	_____
	(B) Pike Master couplers	5	15	_____
(24130)	Pennsylvania Gondola, *60 u*			
	(A) Pike Master couplers	10	26	_____
	(B) Fixed or Operating knuckles	5	16	_____

		Good	Exc	Cond/$
24203	Baltimore & Ohio Hopper, *58, 63–64*			
	(A) Unpainted, *58*	10	25	_____
	(B) Black-painted, *58*		NRS	_____
	(C) PM trucks and couplers, *63–64*	16	60	_____
(24205)	See 921			
24206	CB&Q Hopper, *58*	30	100	_____
(24208)	See 924			
24209	CRP Hopper, *57–60*	30	90	_____
24213	Wabash Hopper, *58–60*	13	48	_____
24216	Union Pacific Hopper, *58–60*	22	80	_____
24219	West. Maryland Hopper, *58–59*	31	130	_____
24221	C&EI Hopper, *59–60*	36	145	_____
24222	Domino Sugars Hopper, *63–64**	135	420	_____
24225	Santa Fe Hopper, *60–65*	10	48	_____
24230	Peabody Hopper, *61–64*			
	(A) Knuckle couplers	21	85	_____
	(B) Pike Master couplers	11	49	_____
(24305)	See 912			
24309	Gulf Tank Car, *57–58*	5	27	_____
24310	Gulf Tank Car, *58–60*	5	20	_____
(24312)	See 926			
24313	Gulf Tank Car, *57–60*	21	80	_____
24316	Mobilgas Tank Car, *57–61, 65–66*			
	(A) Knuckle couplers	15	46	_____
	(B) Pike Master couplers	5	26	_____
24319	PRR Salt Tank Car, *58**	170	600	_____
24320	Deep Rock Tank Car, *60*	130	410	_____
24321	Deep Rock Tank Car, *59*	15	75	_____
24322	Gulf Tank Car, *59*	16	80	_____
24323	Baker's Chocolate Tank Car, *59–60**			
	(A) Type II frame white w/ white ends	500	2000	_____
	(B) Type II frame white w/ gray-painted ends	85	295	_____
	(C) Type III frame white w/ open-bottom tank		NRS	_____
24324	Hooker Tank Car, *59–60*	27	100	_____
24325	Gulf Tank Car, *60*			
	(A) Type II plastic frame	5	20	_____
	(B) Type III plastic frame	15	60	_____
24328	Shell Tank Car, *62–66*	7	20	_____
24329	Hooker Tank Car, *64–65*	10	30	_____
(24329)	Hooker Tank Car, *61–65*	10	40	_____

		Good	Exc	Cond/$
24330	Baker's Chocolate Tank Car, *61–62*	22	70	_____
24403	Illinois Central Reefer, *u**			
	(A) Unpainted	12	23	_____
	(B) Orange painted		—	_____
24409	Northern Pacific Reefer, *58*	400	1400	_____
24413	ART Co. Reefer, *57–60*	42	135	_____
24416	NW Reefer, *58*	720	2250	_____
24419	Canadian National Reefer, *58–59*	100	360	_____
(24420)	Simmons Reefer, *58* u*	1000	1300	_____
24422	Great Northern Boxcars, *63–65, 66 u*	50	140	_____
24422	Great Northern Reefers, *63–65, 66 u*			
	(A) Unpainted green plastic, non-opening door	11	21	_____
	(B) Green-painted plastic, opening door	60	205	_____
	(C) Green-painted plastic, non-opening door	60	205	_____
24425	BAR Reefer, *60*	180	580	_____
24426	Rath Packing Co. Reefer, *60–61*	185	590	_____
24516	New Haven Flatcar, *57–59*	11	33	_____
(24518)	See 936 Pennsylvania			
24519	Pennsylvania Flatcar, *58*	265	1100	_____
(24522)	See 944			
(24525)	See 945			
(24529)	Erie Floodlight, *57–58*	10	50	_____
24533	American Flyer Lines Flatcar, *58–66*	10	41	_____
(24535)	See 956			
24536	Monon Flatcar, *58*	500	1500	_____
24537	New Haven Flatcar, *58 u*	10	46	_____
24539	New Haven Flatcar, *58–59, 63–64*			
	(A) Silver plastic or cardboard pipes, *58–59*	11	41	_____
	(B) Orange cardboard pipes, *63–64*	15	55	_____
24540	New Haven Flatcar, *60 u*	45	180	_____
24543	American Flyer Lines Crane, *58*	10	41	_____
24546	AFL Work and Boom Car, *58–64*	10	40	_____
24547	Erie Floodlight, *58*	195	560	_____
24549	Erie Floodlight, *58–66*			
	(A) Yellow generator, knuckle couplers	13	33	_____
	(B) Red generator	12	32	_____
	(C) Yellow generator, PM couplers	8	22	_____
24550	Monon Flatcar, *59–64*	19	65	_____
24553	Rocket Transport Flatcar, *58–60*	26	95	_____

		Good	Exc	Cond/$
24556	Rock Island Flatcar, *59*	21	80	_____
24557	US Navy Flatcar, *59–61*	33	145	_____
24558	Canadian Pacific Flatcar, *59–60*	70	345	_____
24559	New Haven Flatcar, *59 u*	75	315	_____
24561	American Flyer Lines Crane, *59–61*			
	(A) Gray-painted frame, knuckle couplers, *59*	10	41	_____
	(B) Gray unpainted frame, Pike Master couplers, *60–61*	8	26	_____
24562	New York Central Flatcar, *60*	15	47	_____
(24564)	New Haven Flatcar, *60 u*	10	45	_____
(245)65	FY&PRR Flatcar, *60–61* *	40	165	_____
24566	New Haven Flatcar, *61–64*			
	(A) Black unpainted body	27	85	_____
	(B) Gray unpainted body, *61*	295	940	_____
24566	National Car Co. Flatcar, *61–65*	25	80	_____
24569	AFL Crane, *62–66*	10	24	_____
24572	US Navy Flatcar, *61*	36	145	_____
24574	US Air Force Flatcar, *60–61*			
	(A) Knuckle couplers	41	180	_____
	(B) Pike Master couplers	40	175	_____
24575	National Car Co. Flatcar, *60–66*	17	55	_____
(24575)	Unmarked Borden's Milk Flatcar, *66 u*	10	42	_____
24577	Illinois Central Flatcar, *60–61, 63–64*			
	(A) Pike Master couplers	40	135	_____
	(B) Knuckle couplers	47	155	_____
24578	New Haven Flatcar, *62–63*	90	320	_____
24579	Illinois Central Flatcar, *60–61*	44	175	_____
24603	AFL Caboose, *58*	5	13	_____
(24608)	See 930			
24610	AFL Caboose	6	11	_____
(24618)	See 935			
24619	AFL Bay Window Caboose, *58*	22	95	_____
24626	AFL Caboose, *58*	8	24	_____
24627	AFL Caboose, *59–60*	4	11	_____
24630	AFL Caboose	4	13	_____
24631	American Flyer Lines Caboose, *59–61*	9	33	_____
24632	American Flyer Lines Caboose	30	90	_____
24633	AFL Bay Window Caboose, *59–62*	19	80	_____
24634	AFL Bay Window Caboose, *63–66*	18	55	_____

		Good	Exc	Cond/$
24636	American Flyer Lines Caboose, *61–66*			
	(A) Red	5	12	_____
	(B) Yellow	155	510	_____
24638	AFL Bay Window Caboose, *62*	25	80	_____
(24702)	See 901			
(24705)	See 900			
(24708)	See 902			
(24712)	See 903			
(247)20	FY&PRR Coach, *59–61*			
	(A) Unpainted yellow	20	55	_____
	(B) Yellow painted	25	65	_____
(247)30	FY&PRR Overland Exp. Baggage Car, *59–60*			
	(A) Unpainted yellow	20	55	_____
	(B) Yellow painted	25	65	_____
24733	AFL Pikes Peak Coach, *57*	155	510	_____
24739	AFL Niagara Falls Combination, *57*		NRS	_____
(247)40	Baggage Express Combination, *60*	20	55	_____
(247)50	FY&PRR Combination, *60–61*	50	165	_____
(24772)	See 960			
24773	AFL Columbus Combination Car, *57–58, 60–62*	60	180	_____
(24775)	See 960			
24776	AFL Columbus Combination Car, *59*	60	180	_____
(24792)	See 961			
24793	AFL Jefferson Passenger Car, *57–58, 60–62*	75	235	_____
24794	AFL Jefferson Passenger Car	—	2700	_____
(24795)	See 961			
24796	AFL Jefferson Pullman Car, *59*	60	180	_____
(24812)	See 962			
24813	AFL Hamilton Vista Dome Car, *57–58, 60–62*	60	180	_____
24816	AFL Hamilton Vista Dome Car, *59*	60	180	_____
(24832)	See 963			
24833	AFL Washington Observation Car, *57–58, 60–62*	60	185	_____
(24835)	See 963			
24836	AFL Washington Observation Car, *59*	60	180	_____
24837	Union Pacific Combination Car, *59–60**	100	325	_____
24838	Union Pacific Passenger Car, *59–60**	95	370	_____
24839	Union Pacific Vista Dome Car, *59–60**	95	370	_____
24840	Union Pacific Observation Car, *59–60**	100	325	_____

		Good	Exc	Cond/$
24843	Northern Pacific Combination Car, *58*	90	280	_____
24846	Northern Pacific Passenger Car, *58*	90	280	_____
24849	Northern Pacific Vista Dome Car, *58*	90	280	_____
24853	Northern Pacific Observation Car, *58*	90	280	_____
24856	MoPac Eagle Hill Combination Car, *58, 63–64**	135	500	_____
24859	MoPac Eagle Lake Passenger Car, *58, 63–64**	140	540	_____
24863	MoPac Eagle Creek Passenger Car, *58, 63–64**	130	500	_____
24866	MoPac Eagle Valley Observation Car, *58, 63–64**	125	500	_____
24867	AFL Combination Car, *58 u, 60 u*	50	190	_____
24868	AFL Observation Car, *58 u, 60 u*	50	190	_____
24869	AFL Passenger Car, *58 u, 60 u*	50	190	_____
24963	Car Assortment, *58*		NRS	_____
25003	American Flyer Flatcar, *57–60*	75	275	_____
25005	Mail Car, *57*		NRS	_____
25006	See 918			
(25007)	See 919			
(25012)	See 970			
(25015)	See 971			
25016	Southern Pacific Flatcar, *57–60*	40	140	_____
25018	See 973			
25019	Operating Milk Car, *57–60*	55	110	_____
25025	CB&Q Dump Car, *58–60*	75	235	_____
25031	AFL Caboose, *58*		NRS	_____
(25032)	See 915			
(25033)	See 915			
(25035)	See 979			
25036	See 979			
(25039)	See 978			
25042	Erie Operating Boxcar, *58*	65	200	_____
(25044)	See 969			
25045	Rocket Launcher Flatcar, *57–60*	16	70	_____
25046	Rocket Launcher Flatcar, *60*	15	80	_____
25049	Rio Grande Boxcar, *58–60*	75	260	_____
25052	AFL Bay Window Caboose, *58*	42	160	_____
(25056)	USM and Rocket Launcher set Operating Boxcar and Flatcar, *59*	130	495	_____
25057	TNT Exploding Boxcar, *60*	60	215	_____
25058	Southern Pacific Flatcar, *61–64*	45	145	_____

		Good	Exc	Cond/$
25059	Rocket Launcher Flatcar, *60–64*	20	75	_____
25060	CB&Q Hopper Dump Car, *61–64*	80	275	_____
25061	TNT Exploding Boxcar, *61*	100	330	_____
25062	Mine Carrier Exploding Boxcar, *62–64*	115	360	_____
25071	AF Tie Car Flatcar, *61–64*	7	33	_____
25081	NYC Operating Boxcar, *61–64*	13	46	_____
25082	New Haven Operating Boxcar, *61–64*	10	41	_____
25515	USAF Flatcar, *60–63*	55	195	_____
26101	Curved Track Panel, *65–66*	3	15	_____
26121	Straight Track Panel, *65–66*	5	16	_____
26122	Straight Panel w/ whistle, *65–66*	7	35	_____
26141	Right Switch Panel, *65–66*	7	21	_____
26142	Left Switch Panel, *65–66*	7	21	_____
26151	Crossover Panel, *65–66*	7	16	_____
26300	PM Straight Track, *61–64*	0.10	0.50	_____
26301	PM Straight Track, *61–64*	0.10	0.50	_____
26302	PM Straight Track w/ uncoupler, *61–64*	0.50	3	_____
26310	PM Curved Track, *61–64*	0.10	0.50	_____
26320	PM RH Remote Switch, *61–64*	5	10	_____
26321	PM LH Remote Switch, *61–64*	6	11	_____
26322	PM 90-Degree Crossing, *61–64*	1	3	_____
26323	PM RH Manual Switch, *61–64*	2	6	_____
26324	PM LH Manual Switch, *61–64*	2	6	_____
26340	PM Steel Track Pins, *61–64*	0.40	0.80	_____
26341	PM Insulating Pins, *61–64*	0.40	0.80	_____
26342	PM Adapter Pins, *61–64*	0.30	0.60	_____
26343	PM Track Locks, *61–64*	0.30	0.60	_____
26344	PM Track Terminal, *61–64*	0.20	0.40	_____
26415	Track Assortment, *60, 62*		NRS	_____
26419	Accessory Package, u	5	15	_____
26425	Track Assortment Pack, *60*	6	12	_____
26428	Accessory Pack, *58 u*		NRS	_____
26520	Knuckle Coupler Kit, *57–64*	1	5	_____
26521	Knuckle Coupler Kit, *57–58*		NRS	_____
26601	Fiber Roadbed, *59–62*	0.15	0.75	_____
26602	Fiber Roadbed, *59, 61–62*	0.15	0.75	_____
26670	Track Trip, *57–58*	4	15	_____
26671	Track Trip, *59*	3	10	_____
26672	Track Trip, *60*	2	8	_____
26673	Track Trip, *61–64*	2	8	_____
26690	Track Terminal, w/ envelope, *57–59*	0.50	2	_____
26691	Steel Pins, *57–60, 64*	0.50	1	_____

		Good	Exc	Cond/$
26692	Fiber Pins, *57–60, 64*	0.50	1	_____
26693	Track Locks, dz., *57–60, 64*	2	7	_____
26700	Straight Track, *57–64*	0.15	0.75	_____
26704	Manual uncoupler, u	0.50	1	_____
26708	Horn Control, *57–58*	4	10	_____
26710	Straight Track, *57–64*	0.15	0.60	_____
26718	RC Switch, LH, *57*	7	15	_____
26719	RC Switch, RH, *57*	7	15	_____
26720	Curved Track, *57–64*	0.15	0.60	_____
26722	Curved Track, dz.	6	12	_____
26726	Straight Rubber Roadbed, half section, *58*	1	2	_____
26727	Rubber Roadbed, half section, *58*	1	2	_____
26730	Curved Track, half section, *57–64*	0.15	0.35	_____
26739	Whistle Control, *57–58*	15	45	_____
26742	RC Switches, pair, *57*	10	40	_____
26744	Manual Switches, pair, *57–58*	5	18	_____
26745	Railroad Crossing, *57–64*	1	5	_____
26746	Rubber Roadbed, *57–64*	0.50	1.50	_____
26747	Rubber Roadbed, *57–64*	0.50	1.50	_____
26748	Re-railer, *57–64*	2	7	_____
26749	Bumper, *57–60*	2	13	_____
26751	Pike Planning Kit, *57–59*	8	20	_____
26752	RC Uncoupler, *57–58, 60–61*	1	5	_____
26756	Bumper, *61–64*	5	18	_____
26760	RC Switches, pair, *58–64*	12	40	_____
26761	RC Switch, LH, *58–64*	7	15	_____
26762	RC Switch, RH, *58–64*	7	15	_____
26770	Manual Switches, pair, *59–64*	5	16	_____
26781	Trestle set, *57*	10	25	_____
26782	Trestle set, *58–60*	5	16	_____
26783	Hi-Trestles, *57*	9	22	_____
26790	Trestle set, *61–64*	15	25	_____
26810	Pow-R-Clips, *60–64*	0.20	0.45	_____
27443	Lamps	1	3	_____
27460	Lamp Assortment, *59, 64*	11	27	_____

LIONEL PRODUCTION 1979–2000

0101	See (48712)		
390	See (48472)		
477/478	See (48126/48127)		
479	See (48129)		
480	See (48128)		
491	See (48476)		
591	See (48475)		
625	See (48405)		
0700	NASG Boxcar, *81 u*	110	_____
792	See (48478)		
CZ801	See (48926)		
804-A/804-D	See (48120/48121)		
CZ811	See (48930)		
CZ813	See (48929)		
CZ814	See (48927)		
CZ815	See (48928)		
CZ842	See (48932)		
CZ882	See (48931)		
893	See (48481)		
960	See (48938)		
961	See (48939)		
962	See (48942)		
963	See (48940)		
993	See (48480)		
1094	See (48485)		
1194	See (48486)		
1225	See (48016)		
1261	See (48492)		
1295	See (48494)		
1395	See (48493)		
1496	See (52094)		
1596	See (52095)		
1946-1996	See (48324)		
1990	See (48473)		
1994	See (48487)		
1995	See (48491)		
(2300)	Oil Drum Loader, *83–87*	135	_____
(2321)	Operating Sawmill, *84, 86–87*	130	_____
3993	See (48482)		
5600	See (48013)		
6001/6002	See (48124/48125)		
8000	See (4)8000		

		New	Cond/$
8001	See (4)8001		
8002	See (4)8002		
8005	See (4)8005		
8007	See (4)8007		
8008	See (4)8008		
8009	See (4)8009		
8010	See (4)8010		
8014	See (4)8014		
8100/8101	See (4)8100/(4)8101		
8102/8103	See (4)8102/(4)8103		
8104/8105	See (4)8104/(4)8105		
8106/8107	See (4)8106/(4)8107		
8112/8113	See (4)8112/(4)8113		
8114/8115/8116	See (4)8114/(4)8115/(4)8116		
8117	See (4)8117		
8118	See (4)8118		
8119	See (4)8119		
8123	See (4)8123		
8150/8152	Southern Pacific Alco PA-1 AA set, *81*	375	_____
8151	Southern Pacific Alco PA-1 B Unit, *82*	225	_____
8153/8155	Baltimore & Ohio Alco PA-1 AA set (HARR#1), *81, 83*	360	_____
(8154)	Baltimore & Ohio Alco PA-1 B Unit (HARR#1), *81, 83*	125	_____
8200	See (4)8200		
8201	See (4)8201		
8251/8253	Erie Alco PA-1 AA set, *82*	300	_____
8252	Erie Alco PA-1 B Unit, *82*	130	_____
8308	See (4)8308		
8309	See (4)8309		
8310	See (4)8310		
8311	See (4)8311		
8312	See (4)8312		
8313	See (4)8313		
8314	See (4)8314		
8318	See (4)8318		
8319	See (4)8319		
8321	See (4)8321		
8350	Boston & Maine GP-7 (HARR#2), *83*	360	_____
8403	See (4)8403		
8458	Southern GP-9 (HARR#3), *84*	225	_____
8459	Chessie System GP-20, *84*	305	_____

		New	Cond/$
8460	See (48004)		
8505	See (4)8505		
8551	Santa Fe GP-20, *86*	235	_____
8552	New York Central GP-9 (HARR#4), *86*	215	_____
8553	See (48003)		
8609	See (4)8609		
8681	See (48405)		
8706	See (4)8706		
8707	See (4)8707		
8711	See (4)8711		
8805	See (4)8805		
8806	See (4)8806		
8904	See (4)8904		
8905	See (4)8905		
8906	See (4)8906		
8907	See (4)8907		
8908	See (4)8908		
8909	See (4)8909		
8910	See (4)8910		
8911	See (4)8911		
8912	See (4)8912		
8913	See (4)8913		
8914	See (4)8914		
8915	See (4)8915		
8920	See (4)8920		
8921	See (4)8921		
8922	See (4)8922		
8923	See (4)8923		
8924	See (4)8924		
8925	See (4)8925		
8933	See (4)8933		
8934	See (4)8934		
8941	See (4)8941		
9000	B&O Flatcar w/ trailers (HARR#1), *81, 83*	43	_____
9001	See (4)9001		
9002	B&M Flatcar w/ logs (HARR#2), *83*	80	_____
9003	See (4)9003		
9004	Southern Flatcar w/ trailers (HARR#3), *84*	44	_____
9005	NYC Flatcar w/ trailers (HARR#4), *86*	40	_____
9100	Gulf 1-D Tank Car, *79*	65	_____
9101	Union 76 1-D Tank Car, *80*	35	_____
9102	B&O 1-D Tank Car (HARR#1), *81, 83*	25	_____

		New	Cond/$
9104	B&M 3-D Tank Car (HARR#2), *83*	95	_____
9105	Southern 3-D Tank Car (HARR#3), *84*	30	_____
9106	NYC 3-D Tank Car (HARR#4), *86*	32	_____
9200	Chessie System Hopper w/ coal load, *79*	55	_____
9201	B&O Covered Hopper (HARR#1), *81, 83*	36	_____
9203	Boston & Maine Hopper (HARR#2), *83*	80	_____
9204	Southern Hopper (HARR#3), *84*	27	_____
9205	Pennsylvania Covered Hopper, *84*	45	_____
9206	New York Central Covered Hopper, *84*	30	_____
9207	B&O Covered Hopper, *86*	30	_____
9208	Santa Fe Covered Hopper, *86*	30	_____
9209	New York Central Hopper (HARR#4), *86*	30	_____
9300	Burlington Gondola, *80*	20	_____
9301	B&O Gondola w/ canisters (HARR#1), *81, 83*	21	_____
9303	Southern Gondola w/ canisters (HARR#3), *84*	30	_____
9304	NYC Gondola w/ canisters (HARR#4), *86*	27	_____
9400	Chessie System B/W Caboose, *80*	30	_____
9401	B&O B/W Caboose (HARR#1), *81, 83*	33	_____
9402	B&M B/W Caboose (HARR#2), *83*	90	_____
9403	Southern B/W Caboose (HARR#3), *84*	37	_____
9404	NYC B/W Caboose (HARR#4), *86*	41	_____
9405	Santa Fe B/W Caboose, *86*	35	_____
(9500)	Southern Pacific Combination Car, *81*	110	_____
(9501)	Southern Pacific Passenger Car, *81*	160	_____
(9502)	Southern Pacific Vista Dome Car, *81*	160	_____
(9503)	Southern Pacific Observation Car, *81*	120	_____
9504	Erie Combination Car, *82*	70	_____
9505	Erie Passenger Car, *82*	110	_____
9506	Erie Vista Dome Car, *82*	105	_____
9507	Erie Observation Car, *82*	70	_____
9700	Santa Fe Boxcar, *79*		
	(A) w/ door nibs	—	_____
	(B) w/o door nibs	—	_____
9701	Rock Island Boxcar, *80*	40	_____
9702	Baltimore & Ohio "Sentinel" Boxcar (HARR#1), *81, 83*	50	_____
9703	Boston & Maine Boxcar (HARR #2), *83*	110	_____
9704	Southern Boxcar (HARR#3), *84*	42	_____
9705	Pennsylvania Boxcar, *84*	55	_____
9706	New York Central "Pacemaker" Boxcar, *84*	100	_____
9707	Railbox Boxcar, *84*	70	_____
9708	Conrail Boxcar, *84*	50	_____

		New	Cond/$
9709	Baltimore & Ohio Boxcar, *86*	35	____
9710	Santa Fe Boxcar, *86*	35	____
9711	Southern Pacific Boxcar, *86*	32	____
9712	Illinois Central Gulf Boxcar, *86*	39	____
9713	New York Central Boxcar (HARR#4), *86*	50	____
11492	See (48477)		
20602	See (48479)		
21503	See (48710)		
24063	See (48489)		
24319	See (48402)		
29425	See (48316)		
29426	See (48317)		
31337	See (48498)		
(4)8000	Southern Pacific GP-9 "8000" (HARR#5), *87*	200	____
(4)8001	Illinois Central Gulf GP-20 "8001", *87*	225	____
(4)8002	Southern Pacific GP-9 Dummy "8002" (HARR#5), *88*	165	____
(48003)	Santa Fe GP-20 Dummy "8553", *88*	170	____
(48004)	Chessie System GP-20 Dummy "8460", *88*	170	____
(4)8005	Pennsylvania GP-9 "8005", *89*	220	____
(4)8007	Burlington Northern GP-20 "8007", *90*	300	____
(4)8008	New Haven EP-5 "8008", *91*	225	____
(4)8009	American Flyer GM GP-7 "8009", *91*	200	____
(4)8010	Milwaukee Road EP-5 "8010", *92*	205	____
(48013)	Conrail GP-7 "5600", *95*	225	____
(4)8014	Northern Pacific GP-9 "8014", *95*	250	____
(48016)	Merry Christmas GP-20 "1225", *95*	200	____
48017	Nickel Plate Road GP-9 set "496/497", *97*	360	____
48019	SP GP-20, "4060", *98*	250	____
48020	Milwaukee Road GP-9, "304", *98*	250	____
48021	Conrail SD-40-2 decorated "6381", *98*	NM	____
48022	Conrail SD-40-2 undecorated, *98*	NM	____
(4)8100/(4)8101	Wabash Alco PA-1 AA set "8100/8101" (HARR#6), *88*	320	____
(4)8102/(4)8103	C&O Alco PA-1 AA set "8102/8103" (HARR#7), *89*	270	____
(4)8104/(4)8105	American Flyer RailScope Alco PA-1 AA set "8104/8105", *89–90*	NM	____
(4)8106/(4)8107	UP Alco PA-1 AA set "8106/8107" (HARR#8), *90*	330	____
(4)8112/(4)8113	MoPac Alco PA-1 AA set "8112/8113", *91*	300	____

		New	Cond/$
(4)8114/(4)8115/(4)8116	NP Alco PA-1 ABA set "8114/8115/8116", *92*	425	_____
(4)8117	NP Alco PA-1 B Unit w/ RailSounds "8117", *92*	125	_____
(4)8118	MoPac Alco PA-1 B Unit w/ RailSounds "8118", *92 u*	125	_____
(4)8119	UP Alco PA-1 B Unit w/ RailSounds "8119"(HARR#8), *92 u*	120	_____
(48120/48121)	WP Alco PA-1 AA set "804-A/804-D", *93*	265	_____
(48122)	WP Alco PA-1 B Unit w/ RailSounds, *93*	130	_____
(4)8123	SP Alco PA-1 B Unit w/ RailSounds "8123", *93*	150	_____
(48124/48125)	D&RGW Alco PA-1 AA set "6001/6002", *94*	NM	_____
(48126/48127)	Silver Flash Alco PA-1 AB set "477/478", *95*	CP	_____
(48128)	Silver Flash Alco PA-1 B Unit "480", *95*	72	_____
(48129)	Silver Flash Alco PA-1 A Unit Dummy "479", *96*	108	_____
(48130)	SF Alco PA-1/PB-1 Diesel Locomotives "51-52", *97*	CP	_____
(4)8200	Wabash 4-6-4 "8200" (HARR#6), *88*	NM	_____
(48200)	TCA AT&SF Boxcar, *97*	CP	_____
(4)8201	Santa Fe 4-6-4 "8201", *88*	NM	_____
(48203)	TTOS NYC Reefer, *97*	CP	_____
(48204)	TCA D&RGW Boxcar, *97*	CP	_____
(48205)	NASG Pacific Fruit Express, *97*	CP	_____
(48208)	TCA New England Hopper, *98*	CP	_____
(48209)	TTOS Cotton Belt Boxcar, *98*	CP	_____
(48210)	TCA New England Hopper, *98*	CP	_____
(48211)	NASG Magnolia Tank Car, *98*	CP	_____
48300	Southern Pacific "Overnight" Boxcar (HARR#5), *87*	45	_____
48301	D&RGW Boxcar, *87*	39	_____
48302	Canadian Pacific Boxcar, *87*	34	_____
48303	Chessie System Boxcar, *87*	40	_____
48304	Burlington Northern Boxcar, *87*	50	_____
48305	Wabash Boxcar (HARR#6), *88*	32	_____
48306	Seaboard Coast Line Boxcar, *88*	30	_____
48307	Western Pacific Boxcar, *88*	40	_____
(4)8308	Maine Central Boxcar "8308", *90*	80	_____
(4)8309	Christmas Boxcar "8309", *90 u*	90	_____
(4)8310	MKT Boxcar "8310", *91*	41	_____

		New	Cond/$
(4)8311	Christmas Boxcar "8311", *91 u*	65	____
(4)8312	Missouri Pacific Boxcar "8312", *92*	65	____
(4)8313	BAR "State of Maine" Boxcar "8313", *92*	70	____
(4)8314	Christmas Boxcar "8314", *92 u*	60	____
(48316)	Bangor & Aroostook Reefer "29425", *93*	50	____
(48317)	Rath Packing Reefer "29426", *93*	50	____
(4)8318	A.C. Gilbert Boxcar "8318", *93*	44	____
(4)8319	Christmas Boxcar "8319", *93*	50	____
48320	NKP Boxcar, *94*	40	____
(4)8321	Christmas Boxcar "8321", *94*	45	____
48322	New Haven Boxcar, *95*	41	____
48323	Christmas Boxcar, *95*	41	____
(48324)	AF 50th Anniversary Boxcar "1946-1996", *96*	33	____
48325	Holiday Boxcar, *96*	40	____
(48326)	TCA B&O Boxcar, *96*	CP	____
(48327)	AF Christmas Boxcar "900", *97*	33	____
(48328)	GN Boxcar "900-197", *97*	33	____
(48329)	AT&SF Boxcar "900-297", map graphic, *97*	33	____
(48330)	PRR Boxcar "900-397", *97*	33	____
48332	MKT Boxcar, "937", *98*	40	____
48333	Bangor and Aroostook Boxcar, "982", *98*	40	____
48334	Seaboard Boxcar, "942", *98*	40	____
48335	Christmas 1998 Gondola, *98*	33	____
(48341)	Happy Holidays Boxcar, *99*	CP	____
48400	SP 3-D Tank Car (HARR #5), *87*	40	____
(48402)	Penn Salt 1-D Tank Car "24319", *92*	115	____
(4)8403	British Columbia 1-D Tank Car "8403", *93*	100	____
48404	US Army 1-D Tank Car, *94*	45	____
(48405)	Shell 1-D Tank Car "625" "8681", *95*	CP	____
48406	Celanese Chemicals Tank Car, *96*	36	____
48407	Gilbert Chemicals Tank Car, *96*	36	____
(48408)	Sunoco Single-Dome Tank Car "625", *97*	36	____
(48436)	See (48476)		
48470	NASG Jersey Central Boxcar, *88 u*	125	____
(48471)	NASGMKT 1-D Tank Car "120089", *89 u*	200	____
(48472)	NASG Pennzoil 3-D Tank Car "390", *90 u*	150	____
[48473]	TCA Central of Georgia Boxcar "1990", *90 u*	60	____
(48474)	TCA CNW Reefer "70165", *91 u*	110	____
(48475)	NASG Boraxo Covered Hopper "591", *91 u*	80	____
(48476)	NASG NYC Reefer "491", *91 u*	80	____
(48477)	TCA Ralston-Purina Boxcar "11492", *92 u*	80	____
(48478)	NASG Burlington Boxcar "792", *92 u*	80	____

		New	Cond/$
(48479)	NASG NKP Flatcar w/ Ertl trailer "20602", *92 u*	110	______
(48480)	NASG Susquehanna Boxcar "993", *93 u*	90	______
(48481)	NASG REA Reefer "893", *93 u*	80	______
(48482)	TCA Great Northern Boxcar "3993", *93 u*	80	______
48483	A.C. Gilbert Society "Boys Club" Boxcar, *93 u*	70	______
48484	A.C. Gilbert Society "Boys At The Gate" Boxcar, *93 u*	70	______
(48485)	NASG Northern Pacific Boxcar "1094", *94 u*	65	______
(48486)	NASG NYNH&H Boxcar "1194", *94 u*	65	______
(48487)	TCA Yorkrail Boxcar "1994", *94 u*	110	______
(48490)	TTOS Western Pacific Boxcar "101645", *95 u*	70	______
(48491)	TCA Burlington Northern Flatcar w/ trailers "1995", *95 u*	70	______
(48492)	TCA Northern Pacific Boxcar "1261", *95 u*	70	______
(48493)	NASG Southern Pacific TTUX Flatcars w/ trailers "1395", *95 u*	CP	______
(48494)	NASG Lehigh Valley Covered Grain Hopper "1295", *95 u*	65	______
48495	St. Louis S Gaugers Monsanto 1-D Tank Car, white, *95 u*	100	______
48496	St. Louis S Gaugers Monsanto 1-D Tank Car, orange, *95 u*	495	______
48496	St. Louis S Gaugers Monsanto 1-D Tank Car, orange, *95 u*	495	______
(48497)	TCA MKT 3-D Tank Car "117018", *96 u*	CP	______
(48498)	TTOS Western Pacific Boxcar "31337", *96 u*	CP	______
48500	Southern Pacific Gondola w/ canisters (HARR#5), *87*	30	______
48501	Southern Pacific Flatcar w/ trailers (HARR#5), *87*	40	______
48502	Wabash Flatcar w/ trailers (HARR#6), *88*	40	______
48503	Wabash Gondola w/ canisters (HARR#6), *88*	30	______
(4)8505	Illinois Central Gulf Flatcar w/ bulkheads "8505", *90*	40	______
48507/48508	US Army Flatcars w/ tanks (2), *95*	70	______
48509	AF Equipment Co. Flatcar w/ farm tractors, *95*	41	______
48510	Nickel Plate Road Gondola w/ canisters, *95*	40	______
48511	TTUX Triple Crown Flatcars w/ trailers, *96*	72	______
48513	CSX Flatcar w/ generator, *96*	33	______
(48514)	Intermodal TTUX Set, 2 cars, 2 trailers, *97*	72	______

		New	Cond/$
(48515)	New Haven Flatcar, *99*	CP	
(48516)	SP Searchlight Car "627", *97*	55	
48600	Southern Pacific Hopper (HARR#5), *87*	30	
48601	Union Pacific Covered Hopper, *87*	30	
48602	Erie Covered Hopper, *87*	30	
48603	Wabash Hopper w/ coal load (HARR#6), *88*	30	
48604	Milwaukee Road Covered Hopper, *88*	30	
48605	Burlington Northern Covered Hopper, *88*	30	
(48608)	Domino Sugar Covered Hopper "49608", *92*	70	
(4)8609	D&H Covered Hopper "8609", *93*	45	
48610	NKP Covered Hopper, *94*	36	
48611	Cargill Covered Grain Hopper, *95*	45	
(48612)	ADM 3-Bay Covered Hopper, *97*	36	
48613	B&LE Hoppers 4-pack, *98*	115	
48614	B&LE Hopper, *98*	29	
48700	SP B/W Caboose (HARR#5), *87*	35	
48701	Illinois Central Gulf B/W Caboose, *87*	35	
48702	Wabash S/W Caboose (HARR#6), *88*	36	
48703	Union Pacific S/W Caboose, *88*	40	
48705	Pennsylvania S/W Caboose, *89*	40	
(4)8706	BN S/W Caboose "8706", *90*	45	
(4)8707	NH S/W Caboose "8707", *91*	36	
(48710)	Conrail B/W Caboose "21503", *95*	36	
(4)8711	Northern Pacific B/W Caboose "8711", *95*	40	
(48712)	Happy New Year B/W Caboose "0101", *95*	50	
48713	Nickel Plate Road Caboose, *97*	40	
(48714)	SP Caboose "990", square windows, *97*	40	
(48715)	Milwaukee Road Caboose, *97*	40	
48718	C&NW Caboose, *98*	40	
48719	Conrail Bay Window Caboose, "21137", *98*	40	
48800	Wabash Reefer (HARR#6), *88*	30	
48801	Union Pacific Reefer, *88*	30	
48802	Pennsylvania Reefer, *88*	40	
(4)8805	National Dairy Despatch Insulated Boxcar "8805", *90*	55	
(4)8806	REA Reefer "8806", *94*	40	
48807	NKP Reefer, *94*	40	
48900	C&O Combination Car (HARR#7), *89*	60	
48901	C&O Passenger Car (HARR#7), *89*	70	
48902	C&O Vista Dome Car (HARR#7), *89*	70	
48903	C&O Observation Car (HARR#7), *89*	60	
(4)8904	UP Combination Car "8904" (HARR#8), *90*	60	

		New	Cond/$
(4)8905	UP Passenger Car "8905" (HARR#8), *90*	75	_____
(4)8906	UP Vista Dome Car "8906" (HARR#8), *90*	70	_____
(4)8907	UP Observation Car "8907" (HARR#8), *90*	65	_____
(4)8908	UP Passenger Car "8908" (HARR#8), *90 u*	110	_____
(4)8909	UP Vista Dome Car "8909" (HARR#8), *90 u*	110	_____
(4)8910	MoPac Combination Car "8910", *91*	65	_____
(4)8911	MoPac Vista Dome Car "8911", *91*	65	_____
(4)8912	MoPac Passenger Car "8912", *91*	65	_____
(4)8913	MoPac Observation Car "8913", *91*	65	_____
(4)8914	MoPac Passenger Car "8914", *91*	65	_____
(4)8915	MoPac Vista Dome Car "8915", *91*	65	_____
(4)8920	Northern Pacific Combination Car "8920", *92*	65	_____
(4)8921	Northern Pacific Passenger Car "8921", *92*	65	_____
(4)8922	Northern Pacific Vista Dome Car "8922", *92*	65	_____
(4)8923	Northern Pacific Observation Car "8923", *92*	65	_____
(4)8924	Northern Pacific Vista Dome Car "8924", *92*	65	_____
(4)8925	Northern Pacific Passenger Car "8925", *92*	70	_____
(48926)	WP "California Zephyr" Combination Car "CZ801", *93*	50	_____
(48927)	WP "California Zephyr" Vista Dome Car "CZ814", *93*	55	_____
(48928)	WP "California Zephyr" Vista Dome Car "CZ815", *93*	55	_____
(48929)	WP "California Zephyr" Vista Dome Car "CZ813", *93*	50	_____
(48930)	WP "California Zephyr" Vista Dome Car "CZ811", *93*	50	_____
(48931)	WP "California Zephyr" Observation Car "CZ882", *93*	50	_____
(48932)	WP "California Zephyr" Dining Car "CZ842", *93*	55	_____
(4)8933	MoPac Dining Car "8933", *94*	55	_____
(4)8934	Northern Pacific Dining Car "8934", *94*	60	_____
48935	New Haven Combination Car, *95*	65	_____
48936	New Haven Vista Dome Car, *95*	65	_____
48937	New Haven Observation Car, *95*	65	_____
(48938)	Silver Flash Combination Car "960", *95*	65	_____
(48939)	Silver Flash Passenger Car "961", *95*	65	_____
(48940)	Silver Flash Observation Car "963", *95*	65	_____
(4)8941	Union Pacific Vista Dome Dining Car "8941", *95*	58	_____
(48942)	Vista Dome Car "962", *96*	65	_____
48943	Silver Flash Vista Dome Dining Car, *96*	65	_____
(48944)	AT&SF "Super Chief" Passenger	215	_____

		New	Cond/$
	4-pack "995-98", *97*		
(4)9001	NYC Searchlight Car "9001", *90*	45	_____
(4)9003	Union Pacific Searchlight Car "9003", *91*	45	_____
49006	Milwaukee Road Animated S/W Caboose, *92*	40	_____
49009	AF Lines Flatcar w/ derrick, *96*	36	_____
49010	Stable of Champions Horse Car, *96*	33	_____
(49600)	Union Pacific "Pony Express" set (HARR#8), *90*	630	_____
(49601)	Missouri Pacific "Eagle" set, *91*	550	_____
(49602)	Northern Pacific "North Coast Limited" set, *92*	680	_____
(49604)	Western Pacific "California Zephyr" set, *93*	420	_____
(49605)	New Haven Passenger Car set, *95*	175	_____
(49606)	Silver Flash set, *95*	CP	_____
49608	See (48608)		
(52094)	NASG Ann Arbor Covered Grain Hopper "1496", *96 u*	CP	_____
(52095)	NASG Mobil 1-D Tank Car "1596", *96 u*	CP	_____
70165	See (48474)		
(91653)	National Toy Train Museum Penn Dutch Boxcar	CP	_____
101645	See (48490)		
117018	See (48497)		
120089	See (48471)		

AMERICAN MODELS
1981–2000

Note: All locomotives are AC powered and ready to run unless noted otherwise.

(175)	ICG 40' Boxcar "418388"	30.95	_____
(176)	Reading 40' Boxcar "1104273"	30.95	_____
(177)	ACY 40' Boxcar	30.95	_____
(178)	BN 40' Boxcar "131589"	30.95	_____
(179)	Burlington Route 40' Boxcar "62366"	30.95	_____
(180R)	NP 40' Boxcar "19202"	30.95	_____
(180G)	NP 40' Boxcar "19202"	30.95	_____
(200)	Undecorated 2-bay Hopper, rib-sided	29.95	_____
(201)	C&O 2-bay Hopper, rib-sided	29.95	_____
(202)	WM 2-bay Hopper, rib-sided	29.95	_____
(204)	Erie 2-bay Hopper, rib-sided	29.95	_____
(205)	N&W 2-bay Hopper, rib-sided	29.95	_____
(206)	NYC 2-bay Hopper, rib-sided	29.95	_____
(207)	PRR 2-bay Hopper, rib-sided	29.95	_____
(208)	PEAB 2-bay Hopper, rib-sided	29.95	_____
(209)	Southern 2-bay Hopper, rib-sided	29.95	_____
(210)	UP 2-bay Hopper, rib-sided	29.95	_____
(211)	SP 2-bay Hopper, rib-sided	29.95	_____
(212)	D&RGW 2-bay Hopper, rib-sided	29.95	_____
(213)	Virginian 2-bay Hopper, rib-sided	29.95	_____
(214)	Reading 2-bay Hopper, rib-sided	29.95	_____
(215)	CB&Q 2-bay Hopper, rib-sided	29.95	_____
(216)	LV 2-bay Hopper, rib-sided	29.95	_____
(217)	Interstate 2-bay Hopper, "INT 6012", rib-sided	29.95	_____
(223)	Burlington Route Express 40' Plug Door Boxcar "79225"	30.95	_____
(250)	Undecorated 2-bay Hopper, offset-sided	29.95	_____
(251)	ATSF 2-bay Hopper, offset-sided	29.95	_____
(252)	CP 2-bay Hopper, offset-sided	29.95	_____
(253)	GN 2-bay Hopper, offset-sided	29.95	_____
(254)	NP 2-bay Hopper, offset-sided	29.95	_____
(255)	IC 2-bay Hopper, offset-sided	29.95	_____
(256)	NYC 2-bay Hopper, offset-sided	29.95	_____
(257)	L&N 2-bay Hopper, offset-sided	29.95	_____
(258)	MILW 2-bay Hopper, offset-sided	29.95	_____
(259)	UP 2-bay Hopper, offset-sided	29.95	_____
(260)	SLSF 2-bay Hopper, offset-sided	29.95	_____
(261)	LNE 2-bay Hopper, offset-sided	29.95	_____
(262)	D&H 2-bay Hopper, offset-sided	29.95	_____
(263)	NKP 2-bay Hopper, offset-sided	29.95	_____

		Retail	Cond/$
(264)	MP 2-bay Hopper, offset-sided	29.95	_____
(265)	Conrail 2-bay Hopper, offset-sided	29.95	_____
(266)	CNW 2-bay Hopper, offset-sided	29.95	_____
(267)	Monon 2-bay Hopper, offset-sided	29.95	_____
(268)	B&O 2-bay Hopper, offset-sided	29.95	_____
(500)	Undecorated Tank Car	36.95	_____
(501)	CPC INT Tank Car	36.95	_____
(502)	GATX Tank Car	36.95	_____
(503)	Cargill Tank Car	36.95	_____
(504)	JMHubber Tank Car	36.95	_____
(505)	Englehard Tank Car	36.95	_____
(506)	Georgia Kao Tank Car	36.95	_____
(507)	N.J. Zinc Tank Car	36.95	_____
(508)	BASF Wyand Tank Car	36.95	_____
(509)	American Maize Tank Car	36.95	_____
(510)	B.F. Goodrich Tank Car	36.95	_____
(511)	Elcor Chemical Tank Car	36.95	_____
(512)	Domino Sugar Tank Car	36.95	_____
(1100)	Undecorated 40' Boxcar	30.95	_____
(1100)	WFE 40' Boxcar Premium series	31.95	_____
(1102)	B&O 40' Boxcar	30.95	_____
(1103)	SSW/SP 40' Boxcar	30.95	_____
(1105)	D&RGW 40' Boxcar	30.95	_____
(1105)	BN/WFE 40' Boxcar "76120"	32.95	_____
(1108)	GN 40' Boxcar, Classic series	34.95	_____
(1112)	Soo Line 40' Boxcar	24.95	_____
(1113)	NYC 40' Boxcar	30.95	_____
(1114)	PRR 40' Boxcar	30.95	_____
(1115)	ATSF 40' Boxcar	30.95	_____
(1116)	SEA 40' Boxcar	30.95	_____
(1117)	SP 40' Boxcar	30.95	_____
(1118)	UP 40' Boxcar	30.95	_____
(1119)	C&O 40' Boxcar	30.95	_____
(1121)	NYC 40' Boxcar, Classic series	34.95	_____
(1122)	RUT 40' Boxcar, Classic series	34.95	_____
(1125)	P&LE 40' Boxcar, Premium series	31.95	_____
(1126)	NP40' Boxcar, Premium series	31.95	_____
(1128)	NH 40' Boxcar	30.95	_____
(1129)	GN 40' Boxcar	30.95	_____
(1130)	GM&O 40' Boxcar	30.95	_____
(1131)	N&W 40' Boxcar	30.95	_____
(1132)	CP 40' Boxcar	30.95	_____

		Retail	Cond/$
(1133)	M&StL 40' Boxcar	30.95	_____
(1133)	NYC 40' Boxcar "180454"	30.95	_____
(1134)	Erie-Lack. 40' Boxcar	30.95	_____
(1135)	SP40' Boxcar, Premium series	31.95	_____
(1136)	Susie-Q 40' Boxcar, Classic series	34.95	_____
(1137)	CNW 40' Boxcar	30.95	_____
(1138)	CR 40' Boxcar	30.95	_____
(1500)	Undecorated 50' Ribbed Boxcar	36.95	_____
(1501)	Railbox 50' Ribbed Boxcar	36.95	_____
(1502)	Evergreen 50' Ribbed Boxcar	36.95	_____
(1503)	MEC 50' Ribbed Boxcar	36.95	_____
(1504)	CNW 50' Ribbed Boxcar	36.95	_____
(1505)	UP 50' Ribbed Boxcar	39.95	_____
(1506)	Conrail 50' Ribbed Boxcar	36.95	_____
(1507)	BN 50' Ribbed Boxcar	36.95	_____
(1508)	Tropicana 50' Ribbed Boxcar	36.95	_____
(1509)	D&RGW 50' Ribbed Boxcar	36.95	_____
(1510)	Rail Link 50' Ribbed Boxcar	36.95	_____
(1511)	CSX Link 50' Ribbed Boxcar	36.95	_____
(2200)	Undecorated 40' Plug Door Boxcar	30.95	_____
(2202)	PFE 40' Boxcar, Premium series	32.95	_____
(2203)	ART 40' Boxcar, Premium series	32.95	_____
(2204)	PGE 40' Boxcar, Premium series	32.95	_____
(2206)	Dubuque 40' Boxcar, Premium series	32.95	_____
(2207)	WP 40' Plug Door Boxcar	30.95	_____
(2208)	CN 40' Plug Door Boxcar	30.95	_____
(2209)	DT&I 40' Boxcar, Premium series	34.95	_____
(2210)	ATSF 40' Boxcar, Premium series	34.95	_____
(2211)	PRR 40' Plug Door Boxcar	30.95	_____
(2212)	Soo Line 40' Plug Door Boxcar	30.95	_____
(2213)	MILW 40' Plug Door Boxcar	30.95	_____
(2215)	NYC 40' Boxcar, Premium series	34.95	_____
(2216)	BN 40' Boxcar, Premium series	34.95	_____
(2217)	GN 40' Plug Door Boxcar	30.95	_____
(2218)	CP 40' Plug Door Boxcar	30.95	_____
(2219)	PG&E 40' Plug Door Boxcar	30.95	_____
(2220)	B&A 40' Boxcar Classic series	33.95	_____
(2221)	NP 40' Boxcar Classic series	33.95	_____
(2222)	Miller 40' Plug Door Boxcar	30.95	_____
(3300)	Undecorated PS-2 CD 3-bay Hopper	39.95	_____
(3301)	A.D.M. PS-2 CD 3-bay Hopper "2114"	39.95	_____
(3302)	BN PS-2 CD 3-bay Hopper "450995"	39.95	_____

		Retail	Cond/$
(3303)	Cargill PS-2 CD 3-bay Hopper "TLDX 2520"	39.95	_____
(3304)	C&NW PS-2 CD 3-bay Hopper "96758"	39.95	_____
(3305)	Conrail PS-2 CD 3-bay Hopper "865781"	39.95	_____
(3306)	GN PS-2 CD 3-bay Hopper "172213"	39.95	_____
(3307)	IC PS-2 CD 3-bay Hopper "54607"	39.95	_____
(3308)	PRR PS-2 CD 3-bay Hopper "260084"	39.95	_____
(3309)	Pillsbury PS-2 CD 3-bay Hopper "3089"	39.95	_____
(3310)	D&RGW PS-2 CD 3-bay Hopper "15045"	39.95	_____
(3311)	The Rock PS-2 CD 3-bay Hopper "13278"	39.95	_____
(3312)	AT&SF PS-2 CD 3-bay Hopper "304227"	39.95	_____
(3313)	UP PS-2 CD 3-bay Hopper "21753"	39.95	_____
(3400)	Undecorated 4-bay Hopper	33.95	_____
(3401)	B&O 4-bay Hopper "532161"	33.95	_____
(3402)	C&O 4-bay Hopper "67297"	33.95	_____
(3403)	IC 4-bay Hopper "67049"	33.95	_____
(3404)	NH 4-bay Hopper "81225"	33.95	_____
(3405)	MP 4-bay Hopper "1912"	33.95	_____
(3406)	Peabody Coal 4-bay Hopper "8676"	33.95	_____
(3407)	Rock Island 4-bay Hopper "133288"	33.95	_____
(3408)	AT&SF 4-bay Hopper "181040"	33.95	_____
(3409)	WM 4-bay Hopper "15308"	33.95	_____
(3410)	NYC 4-bay Hopper "904641"	33.95	_____
(3451)	BN 4-bay Hopper "514024"	33.95	_____
(3452)	C&BQ 4-bay Hopper "171426"	33.95	_____
(3453)	C&NW 4-bay Hopper "64651"	33.95	_____
(3454)	CR 4-bay Hopper "403122"	33.95	_____
(3455)	CSX 4-bay Hopper "311566"	33.95	_____
(3456)	D&RGW 4-bay Hopper "12543"	33.95	_____
(3457)	GN 4-bay Hopper "705014"	33.95	_____
(3458R)	PRR 4-bay Hopper "923678"	33.95	_____
(3458B)	GN 4-bay Hopper "918295"	33.95	_____
(3459)	UP 4-bay Hopper "901423"	33.95	_____
(3460)	SP 4-bay Hopper "43277"	33.95	_____
(3461)	Virginian 4-bay Hopper "9059"	33.95	_____
(4400)	Undecorated Gondola	30.95	_____
(4401)	SLSF Gondola	30.95	_____
(4401)	Frisco Gondola "61760"	30.95	_____
(4402)	Wabash Gondola	30.95	_____
(4402)	BN Gondola "565557"	30.95	_____
(4403)	Southern Gondola	30.95	_____

		Retail	Cond/$
(4404)	PRR Gondola	30.95	_____
(4405)	GN Gondola	30.95	_____
(4406)	LV Gondola	30.95	_____
(4407)	B&O Gondola	30.95	_____
(4408)	C&O Gondola	30.95	_____
(4409)	MILW Gondola	30.95	_____
(4410)	SP Gondola	30.95	_____
(4411)	WM Gondola	30.95	_____
(4412)	Soo Line Gondola	30.95	_____
(4413)	Lackawanna Gondola	30.95	_____
(4414)	IC Gondola	30.95	_____
(4415)	NYC Gondola	30.95	_____
(4416)	NKP Gondola	30.95	_____
(4417)	N&W Gondola	30.95	_____
(4418)	UP Gondola	30.95	_____
(4419)	ATSF Gondola	30.95	_____
(4420)	BN Gondola	30.95	_____
(4421)	CP Gondola	30.95	_____
(4422)	NP Gondola	30.95	_____
(4423)	D&H Gondola	30.95	_____
(4424)	Reading Gondola	30.95	_____
(4425)	D&RGW Gondola	30.95	_____
(4426)	CNW Gondola	30.95	_____
(4427)	CR Gondola	30.95	_____
(4428)	MP Gondola	30.95	_____
(7700)	Undecorated Caboose	36.95	_____
(7701)	Chessie Caboose	36.95	_____
(7702)	Erie Caboose	36.95	_____
(7703)	Erie-Lack. Caboose, red	36.95	_____
(7704)	Conrail Caboose	36.95	_____
(7705)	CNW Caboose	36.95	_____
(7705)	Southern Caboose	36.95	_____
(7707)	NYC Caboose	36.95	_____
(7708)	PRR Caboose	36.95	_____
(7709)	NW Caboose	36.95	_____
(7710)	ATSF Caboose	36.95	_____
(7711)	SP Caboose	36.95	_____
(7712)	GN Caboose	36.95	_____
(7713)	NP Caboose	36.95	_____
(7714)	UP Caboose	36.95	_____
(7715)	NH Caboose	36.95	_____
(7716)	CP Caboose	36.95	_____

		Retail	Cond/$
(7718)	Erie-Lackawanna Caboose, maroon and gray	38.95	_____
(7719)	BN Caboose	36.95	_____
(7720)	Burlington Caboose "1113"	38.95	_____
(46000)	Undecorated USRA 4-6-2	—	_____
(46001)	B&O USRA 4-6-2	—	_____
(46002)	Southern USRA 4-6-2	—	_____
(46500)	Undecorated USRA 4-6-2	—	_____
(46501)	B&O USRA 4-6-2	—	_____
(46502)	Southern USRA 4-6-2	—	_____
(BSSC1)	Conrail Trailer Hauler Freight set	299.95	_____
(BSSC4)	SP Trailer Hauler Freight set	299.95	_____
(CB208S)	Ground Throw	2.70	_____
(F40P2)	Amtrak EMD F-40 PH-2	199.95	_____
(F40P3)	Amtrak EMD F-40 PH-3	199.95	_____
(FA2000)	Undecorated Alco FA-2	189.95	_____
(FA2001)	CP Alco FA-2	189.95	_____
(FA2002)	GN Alco FA-2	189.95	_____
(FA2003)	NH Alco FA-2 "10401"	189.95	_____
(FA2004)	NYC Alco FA-2	189.95	_____
(FA2005)	UP Alco FA-2	189.95	_____
(FA2006)	PRR Alco FB-2	189.95	_____
(FB2000)	Undecorated Alco FB-2	189.95	_____
(FB2001)	CP Alco FB-2	189.95	_____
(FB2002)	GN Alco FB-2	189.95	_____
(FB2003)	NH Alco FB-2	189.95	_____
(FB2004)	NYC Alco FB-2	189.95	_____
(FB2005)	UP Alco FB-2	189.95	_____
(FB2006)	PRR Alco FB-2	189.95	_____
(FB7000)	Undecorated EMD FB-7	189.95	_____
(FB7001)	BN EMD FB-7	189.95	_____
(FB7002)	GN EMD FB-7	189.95	_____
(FB7003)	NYC EMD FB-7	189.95	_____
(FB7004)	NP EMD FB-7	189.95	_____
(FB7005)	PRR EMD FB-7, tuscan	189.95	_____
(FB7006)	PRR EMD FB-7, green	189.95	_____
(FB7007)	SP EMD FB-7	189.95	_____
(FB7008)	UP EMD FB-7	189.95	_____
(FP7000)	Undecorated EMD FP-7	189.95	_____
(FP7001)	BN EMD FP-7	189.95	_____
(FP7002)	GN EMD FP-7	189.95	_____
(FP7003)	NYC EMD FP-7	189.95	_____

	Retail	Cond/$
(FP7004) NP EMD FP-7	189.95	_____
(FP7005) PRR EMD FP-7, tuscan	189.95	_____
(FP7006) PRR EMD FP-7, green	189.95	_____
(FP7007) SP EMD FP-7	189.95	_____
(FP7008) UP EMD FP-7	189.95	_____
(GG1200) Undecorated GG-1 Electric	309.95	_____
(GG1201) PRR GG-1 Electric, green	309.95	_____
(GG1202) PRR GG-1 Electric, tuscan	309.95	_____
(GP9000) Undecorated EMD GP-9	189.95	_____
(GP9001) Conrail EMD GP-9	189.95	_____
(GP9002) Erie-Lack. EMD GP-9	189.95	_____
(GP9003) NH EMD GP-9	189.95	_____
(GP9004) NYC EMD GP-18 "5918"	189.95	_____
(GP9005) N&W EMD GP-9	189.95	_____
(GP9006) PRR EMD GP-9	189.95	_____
(GP9007) ATSF EMD GP-9	189.95	_____
(GP9008) SP EMD GP-9	189.95	_____
(GP9009) UP EMD GP-9	189.95	_____
(GP9010) C&O EMD GP-9	189.95	_____
(GP35000) Undecorated EMD GP-35	189.95	_____
(GP35001) C&O EMD GP-35	189.95	_____
(GP35002) CNW EMD GP-35	199.95	_____
(GP35003) Conrail EMD GP-35	199.95	_____
(GP35004) Erie-Lack. EMD GP-35	189.95	_____
(GP35005) GN EMD GP-35	199.95	_____
(GP35006) MP EMD GP-35	189.95	_____
(GP35007) NYC EMD GP-35	189.95	_____
(GP35008) PRR EMD GP-35	189.95	_____
(GP35010) SP EMD GP-35	199.95	_____
(GP35011) UP EMD GP-35	199.95	_____
(GP35012) BN EMD GP-35	199.95	_____
(GP35013) CSX EMD GP-35	209.95	_____
(GP35014) ATSF EMD GP-35, warbonnet	209.95	_____
(GP35015) Soo Line EMD GP-35	189.95	_____
(GP35016) D&RGW EMD GP-35	199.95	_____
(GP35017) Ann Harbor EMD GP-35 "383"	189.95	_____
(HA8000) Undecorated 80' Passenger Lightweight Streamline set	249.95	_____
(HA8001) GN 80' Passenger Lightweight Streamline set	249.95	_____
(HA8002) NP 80' Passenger Lightweight Streamline set	249.95	_____

		Retail	Cond/$
(HA8003)	NYC 80' Passenger Lightweight Streamline set	249.95	_____
(HA8004)	PRR 80' Passenger Lightweight Streamline set	249.95	_____
(HA8006)	UP 80' Passenger Lightweight Streamline set	249.95	_____
(HA8100)	Undecorated Baggage-Dormitory	44.95	_____
(HA8101)	NP Baggage-Dormitory	44.95	_____
(HA8103)	NYC Baggage-Dormitory	44.95	_____
(HA8104)	PRR Baggage-Dormitory	44.95	_____
(HA8106)	UP Baggage-Dormitory	44.95	_____
(HA8111)	GN Baggage-Dormitory	44.95	_____
(HA8200)	Undecorated 60-seat Coach	44.95	_____
(HA8201)	NP 60-seat Coach	44.95	_____
(HA8203)	NYC 60-seat Coach	44.95	_____
(HA8204)	PRR 60-seat Coach	44.95	_____
(HA8206)	UP 60-seat Coach	44.95	_____
(HA8211)	GN 60-seat Coach	44.95	_____
(HA8300)	Undecorated Vista Dome	44.95	_____
(HA8301)	NP Vista Dome	44.95	_____
(HA8303)	NYC Vista Dome	44.95	_____
(HA8304)	PRR Vista Dome	44.95	_____
(HA8306)	UP Vista Dome	44.95	_____
(HA8311)	GN Vista Dome	44.95	_____
(HA8400)	Undecorated 4-16 Duplex Sleeper	44.95	_____
(HA8401)	NP 4-16 Duplex Sleeper	44.95	_____
(HA8403)	NYC 4-16 Duplex Sleeper	44.95	_____
(HA8404)	PRR 4-16 Duplex Sleeper	44.95	_____
(HA8406)	UP 4-16 Duplex Sleeper	44.95	_____
(HA8411)	GN 4-16 Duplex Sleeper	44.95	_____
(HA8500)	Undecorated Observation Lounge	44.95	_____
(HA8501)	NP Observation Lounge	44.95	_____
(HA8503)	NYC Observation Lounge	44.95	_____
(HA8504)	PRR Observation Lounge	44.95	_____
(HA8506)	UP Observation Lounge	44.95	_____
(HA8511)	GN Observation Lounge	44.95	_____
(HW8000)	Undecorated 72' Heavyweight Passenger set	289.95	_____
(HW8001)	NW 72' Heavyweight Passenger set,	289.95	_____
(HW8003)	UP 72' Heavyweight Passenger set	289.95	_____
(HW8004)	NH 72' Heavyweight Passenger set	289.95	_____
(HW8005)	NYC 72' Heavyweight Passenger set	289.95	_____

	Retail	Cond/$
(HW8006) ATSF 72' Heavyweight Passenger set,	289.95	_____
(HW8007) D&RGW 72' Heavyweight Passenger set	289.95	_____
(HW8008) C&NW 72' Heavyweight Passenger set	289.95	_____
(HW8009) PRR 72' Heavyweight Passenger set	289.95	_____
(HW8010) PRR 72' Heavyweight Passenger set w/Pullman	289.95	_____
(HW8012) SP 72' Heavyweight Passenger set	289.95	_____
(HW8200) Undecorated Heavyweight Coach	59.95	_____
(HW8201) CNW Heavyweight Coach	59.95	_____
(HW8203) UP Heavyweight Coach	59.95	_____
(HW8204) NH Heavyweight Coach	59.95	_____
(HW8205) NYC Heavyweight Coach	59.95	_____
(HW8206) ATSF Heavyweight Coach	59.95	_____
(HW8207) D&RGW Heavyweight Coach	59.95	_____
(HW8209) PRR Heavyweight Coach	59.95	_____
(HW8210) PRR Heavyweight Coach w/ Pullman,	59.95	_____
(HX8100) Undecorated 80' Pullman Heavyweight 12-1 Sleeper	55	_____
(HX8200) Undecorated 80' Pullman Heavyweight 10-1 Sleeper	55	_____
(HX8300) Undecorated 80' Pullman Heavyweight Cafe	55	_____
(LTD RUN) Wisconsin Central EMD GP-35 "728",	219.95	_____
(PABA400) Undecorated Alco PA-1 ABA set	550	_____
(PABA401) PRR Alco PA-1 ABA set, freight scheme, green	550	_____
(PABA402) ATSF Alco PA-1 ABA set, warbonnet scheme, tuscan	550	_____
(PABA403) NYC Alco PA-1 ABA set	550	_____
(PABA404) NYC Alco PA-2 ABA set	550	_____
(PABA405) NYC System Alco PA-1 ABA set	550	_____
(PABA406) D&RGW Alco PA-1 ABA set	550	_____
(PABA407) NH McGuiness scheme Alco PA-1 ABA set	550	_____
(PABA408) UP Alco PA-1 ABA set	550	_____
(PABA409) ATSF Alco PA-1 ABA set, warbonnet scheme	550	_____
(PABA410) ATSF Alco PA-1 ABA set, freight scheme	550	_____
(PABA411) D&H Alco PA-1 ABA set	550	_____
(PABA412) SP Daylight Alco PA-1 ABA set "6055"	585	_____
(RS3000) Undecorated Alco RS-3	189.95	_____
(RS3001) Conrail Alco RS-3	189.95	_____
(RS3002) SSW/SP Alco RS-3	189.95	_____

		Retail	Cond/$
(RS3003)	EL Alco RS-3	189.95	_____
(RS3004)	GN Alco RS-3	189.95	_____
(RS3005)	NH Alco RS-3	189.95	_____
(RS3006)	NYC Alco RS-3	189.95	_____
(RS3007)	PRR Alco RS-3	189.95	_____
(S1200)	Undecorated Baldwin S-12	199.95	_____
(S1201)	NH Baldwin S-12	209.95	_____
(S1202)	CNW Baldwin S-12	209.95	_____
(S1203)	Conrail Baldwin S-12	199.95	_____
(S1204)	Erie-Lack. Baldwin S-12	214.95	_____
(S1206)	Southern Baldwin S-12	219.95	_____
(S1207)	NYC Baldwin S-12	199.95	_____
(S1208)	PRR Baldwin S-12	199.95	_____
(S1209)	ATSF Baldwin S-12	214.95	_____
(S1210)	SP Baldwin S-12	209.95	_____
(S1211)	UP Baldwin S-12	209.95	_____
(S1212)	DRG Baldwin S-12	214.95	_____
(S1214)	BN Baldwin S-12	214.95	_____
(S1215)	BN Baldwin S-12	199.95	_____
(S1219)	B&O Baldwin S-12	199.95	_____
(S1220)	IC Baldwin S-12	209.95	_____
(S1222)	CP Baldwin S-12	214.95	_____
(S1224)	SP Baldwin S-12 "106"	214.95	_____
(SC65T)	Trailer Train 5-unit Spine set w/ trailer	159.95	_____
(SLBSP2)	Amtrak Superliner set, Phase II	369.95	_____
(T-1)	UP 40' Semi Trailer "Trailer Freight Service"	11.95	_____
(T-2)	SOU 40' Semi Trailer "700425"	11.95	_____
(T-3)	BN 40' Semi Trailer "BNZ 233304"	11.95	_____
(T-4)	CSX 40' Semi Trailer "580Z231008"	11.95	_____
(T-5)	D&RGW 40' Semi Trailer "RRGZ 201077"	11.95	_____
(T-6)	AT&SF 40' Semi Trailer	11.95	_____
(T-7)	SP 40' Semi Trailer	11.95	_____
(T-8)	Quantum 40' Semi Trailer "HSFZ610007"	11.95	_____
(T-9)	IC 40' Semi Trailer	11.95	_____
(T-10)	CN&W 40' Semi Trailer	11.95	_____
(T-11)	Conrail 40' Semi Trailer	11.95	_____
(T-12)	American President Line 40' Semi Trailer	11.95	_____
(T-13)	K-Line 40' Semi Trailer	11.95	_____
(T-14)	Evergreen 40' Semi Trailer	11.95	_____
(T-15)	N&W 40' Semi Trailer "TCSZ216380"	11.95	_____
(T-16)	Transamerica 40' Semi Trailer "TDSZ500035"	11.95	_____

		Retail	Cond/$
(T-17)	MP 40' Semi Trailer "MPZ20322"	11.95	_____
(T-18)	SP 40' Semi Trailer "SPLZ731908"	11.95	_____
(T148L)	LH 27" Radius Track	17.98	_____
(T148R)	RH 27" Radius Track	17.98	_____
(T710)	Rail Joiners (36)	2.25	_____
(T711)	Terminal w/ wire	1.50	_____
(T14812)	12" Straight Track	2.98	_____
(T14821)	21" Radius S-42 Track	3.08	_____
(T14824)	24" Radius S-48 Track	3.28	_____
(T14827)	27" Radius S-54 Track	3.28	_____
(T14836)	3' Flex Track	7.50	_____
(TWS103)	Rail Weathering Solution (3 oz.)	6	_____

S-HELPER SERVICE
1994–2000

(00001)	70-ton FB Truck, code 110, *94–98*	5.95	_____
(00002)	70-ton FB Truck, hi-rail, *94–98*	5.95	_____
(00003)	70-ton RB Truck, code 110, *94–98*	5.95	_____
(00004)	70-ton RB Truck, hi-rail, *94–98*	5.95	_____
(00005)	Hi-rail Freight Coupler, pair, *94–98*	2.95	_____
(00006)	B&M PS-2 Covered Hopper, "5541", *94–95*	39.95	_____
(00007)	NYC PS-2 Covered Hopper, "573251", *94–95*	39.95	_____
(00008)	PRR PS-2 Covered Hopper, "257701", *94–95*	39.95	_____
(00009)	SF PS-2 Covered Hopper, "87421", *94–95*	39.95	_____
(00010)	Wabash PS-2 Covered Hopper, "30321", *94–95*	39.95	_____
(00011)	WM PS-2 Covered Hopper, "5531", *94–95*	39.95	_____
(00012)	BN PS-2 Covered Hopper, "42471", *94–95*	39.95	_____
(00013)	Chessie-WM PS-2 Covered Hopper, "5861", *94–95*	39.95	_____
(00014)	CNW PS-2 Covered Hopper, "70551", *94–95*	39.95	_____
(00015)	Conrail PS-2 Covered Hopper, "877351", *94–95*	39.95	_____
(00016)	Soo Line PS-2 Covered Hopper, "69091", *94–95*	39.95	_____
(00017)	SP PS-2 Covered Hopper, "401431", *94–96*	39.95	_____
(00018)	CNJ PS-2 Covered Hopper, "751", *94–96*	39.95	_____
(00019)	MILW PS-2 Covered Hopper, "99631", *94–96*	39.95	_____
(00020)	Trona PS-2 Covered Hopper, "31053", *94*	39.95	_____
(00021)	Unlettered PS-2 Covered Hopper, friction bearing, gray, *94–96*	39.95	_____
(00022)	PRR PS-2 Covered Hopper, "257781", *94–95*	39.95	_____
(00023)	S-2 RB Truck 36", code 110, *94–98*	39.95	_____
(00024)	33" Scale Wheelsets, four pack, *94–98*	3.95	_____
(00025)	33" hi-rail Wheelsets, four pack, *94–98*	3.95	_____
(00026)	PRR PS-2 Covered Hopper, "257862", sm. keystone, *94*	39.95	_____
(00027)	B&O PS-2 Covered Hopper, "631512", *95–96*	39.95	_____
(00028)	D&RGW PS-2 Covered Hopper, "18332", *95–96*	39.95	_____
(00029)	SF PS-2 Covered Hopper, "82412", scheme #2, *95–96*	39.95	_____
(00030)	MEC PS-2 Covered Hopper, "2492", *95–96*	39.95	_____
(00031)	UP PS-2 Covered Hopper, "11561", *95–96*	39.95	_____
(00032)	WC PS-2 Covered Hopper, "81152", *95–96*	39.95	_____
(00033)	LV PS-2 Covered Hopper, "50772", *95–96*	39.95	_____
(00034)	RI PS-2 Covered Hopper, "507102", scheme #1, *95*	39.95	_____

		Retail	Cond/$
(00035)	RI PS-2 Covered Hopper, "507182", scheme #2, *95*	39.95	_____
(00036)	DT&I PS-2 Covered Hopper, "11186", *95–96*	39.95	_____
(00037)	CSX PS-2 Covered Hopper, "22606L", *95–96*	39.95	_____
(00038)	CNW/CNW PS-2 Covered Hopper, "95242", scheme #2, *95*	39.95	_____
(00039)	CNW/CGW PS-2 Covered Hopper, "7232", *95*	39.95	_____
(00040)	BN PS-2 Covered Hopper, "424702", *95*	39.95	_____
(00041)	DT&I PS-2 Covered Hopper, "11196", scheme #2, *95–96*	39.95	_____
(00042)	IMCO PS-2 Covered Hopper, "41012", *95*	39.95	_____
(00043)	Unlettered PS-2 Covered Hopper, roller bearing, gray, *95*	39.95	_____
(00044)	Chessie/B&O PS-2 Covered Hopper, "631542", *95–96*	39.95	_____
(00045)	50-ton Andrews Truck, code 110, *96–98*	5.95	_____
(00046)	50-ton Andrews Truck, hi-rail, *96–98*	5.95	_____
(00047)	50-ton 2D-F8 Truck, code 110, *96–98*	5.95	_____
(00048)	50-ton 2D-F8 Truck, hi-rail, *96–98*	5.95	_____
(00049)	Unlettered Stock Car, red, *96*	39.95	_____
(00050)	UP Stock Car, "49001", scheme #1, *96*	39.95	_____
(00051)	UP Stock Car, "49042", scheme #2, *96*	39.95	_____
(00052)	Rio Grande Stock Car, "36491", *96*	39.95	_____
(00053)	CNW Stock Car, "14201", scheme #1, *96*	39.95	_____
(00054)	CNW Stock Car, "14252", scheme #2, *96*	39.95	_____
(00055)	ACL Stock Car, "140441", *96*	39.95	_____
(00056)	GN Stock Car, "53051", scheme #1, *96*	39.95	_____
(00057)	GN Stock Car, "53083", scheme #2, *96*	39.95	_____
(00058)	PRR Stock Car, "1218121", scheme #1, *96*	39.95	_____
(00059)	PRR Stock Car, "1219172", scheme #2, *96*	39.95	_____
(00060)	SF Stock Car, "23001", scheme #1, *96*	39.95	_____
(00061)	SF Stock Car, "23062", scheme #2, *96*	39.95	_____
(00062)	NP Stock Car, "24001", *96*	39.95	_____
(00063)	Unlettered USRA Wooden Boxcar, red, *96*	39.95	_____
(00064)	NYC Stock Car, "22591", *96*	39.95	_____
(00065)	WP Stock Car, "75891", *96*	39.95	_____
(00066)	PRR USRA Wooden Boxcar, "564281", #1, *96*	39.95	_____
(00067)	PRR USRA Wooden Boxcar, "518392", #2, *96*	39.95	_____
(00068)	CB&Q/C&S USRA Wooden Boxcar, "13501", *96*	39.95	_____
(00069)	CB&Q/CB&Q USRA Wooden Boxcar, "25321", *96*	39.95	_____

(00070)	MEC/PTM USRA Wooden Boxcar, "2081", *96*	39.95	_____
(00071)	B&O USRA Wooden Boxcar, "167051", *96*	39.95	_____
(00072)	SP USRA Wooden Boxcar, "26541", *96*	39.95	_____
(00073)	NYC USRA Wooden Boxcar, "277361", *96*	39.95	_____
(00074)	NMRA-GG, YV&N USRA Wooden Boxcar, "77569", *96*	39.95	_____
(00075)	CP USRA Wooden Boxcar, "230471", *96*	39.95	_____
(00076)	GN PS-2 Covered Hopper, "71451", *96*	39.95	_____
(00077)	NKP PS-2 Covered Hopper, "905003", *96*	39.95	_____
(00078)	PL&E (NYC) PS-2 Covered Hopper, "1563", *96*	39.95	_____
(00079)	Soo Line PS-2 Covered Hopper, "6873", scheme #2, *96*	39.95	_____
(00080)	New Haven PS-2 Covered Hopper, "117093", *96*	39.95	_____
(00081)	WP PS-2 Covered Hopper, "11203", *96*	39.95	_____
(00082)	MKT PS-2 Covered Hopper, "1333", *96*	39.95	_____
(00083)	BN PS-2 Covered Hopper, "424723", *96*	39.95	_____
(00084)	PC PS-2 Covered Hopper, "74202", *96*	39.95	_____
(00085)	Chessie (CSXT) PS-2 Covered Hopper, "226403", *96*	39.95	_____
(00086)	CNW/CNW PS-2 Covered Hopper, "69473", *96*	39.95	_____
(00087)	Revere Sugar PS-2 Covered Hopper, "133", *96*	39.95	_____
(00088)	Conrail PS-2 Covered Hopper, "877353", scheme #2, *96*	39.95	_____
(00089)	Grand Trunk PS-2 Covered Hopper, "111163", *96*	39.95	_____
(00090)	Ready Mix Concrete PS-2 Covered Hopper, "326", *96*	39.95	_____
(00091)	SP PS-2 Covered Hopper, "402243" scheme #2, *96*	39.95	_____
(00092)	Unlettered SW-9, black, *97*	199.95	_____
(00093)	ACL SW-9, "701", scheme #1, *97*	199.95	_____
(00094)	ACL SW-9 "652", scheme #2, *97*	199.95	_____
(00095)	Amtrak SW-9, scheme #1, *97*	199.95	_____
(00096)	Amtrak SW-9, scheme #2, *97*	199.95	_____
(00097)	B&O SW-9 "9611", scheme #1, *97*	199.95	_____
(00098)	B&O SW-9 "9612", scheme #2, *97*	199.95	_____
(00099)	B&M SW-9 "1231", scheme #1, *97*	199.95	_____
(00100)	B&M SW-9 "1222", scheme #2, *97*	199.95	_____
(00101)	BN SW-9 "161", scheme #1, *97*	199.95	_____
(00102)	BN SW-9 "169", scheme #2, *97*	199.95	_____
(00103)	CP SW-9 "7401", scheme #1, *97*	199.95	_____

		Retail	Cond/$
(00104)	CP SW-9 "7405", scheme #2, *97*	199.95	_____
(00105)	CB&Q SW-9 "9269", scheme #1, *97*	199.95	_____
(00106)	CB&Q SW-9 "9270", scheme #2, *97*	199.95	_____
(00107)	Chessie System SW-9 "C&O", scheme #1, *97*	199.95	_____
(00108)	Chessie System SW-9 "WM", scheme #2, *97*	199.95	_____
(00109)	CNW SW-9 "1101", scheme #1, *97*	199.95	_____
(00110)	CNW SW-9 "1102", scheme #2, *97*	199.95	_____
(00111)	Conrail SW-9, scheme #1, *97*	199.95	_____
(00112)	Conrail SW-9, scheme #2, *97*	199.95	_____
(00113)	Erie Lack. SW-9 "451", scheme #1, *97*	199.95	_____
(00114)	Erie Lack. SW-9 "452", scheme #2, *97*	199.95	_____
(00115)	NYC SW-9 "8971", scheme #1, *97*	199.95	_____
(00116)	NYC SW-9 "8922", scheme #2, *97*	199.95	_____
(00117)	PRR SW-9 "8531", scheme #1, *97*	199.95	_____
(00118)	PRR SW-9 "8522", scheme #2, *97*	199.95	_____
(00119)	SF SW-9 "2421", scheme #1, *97*	199.95	_____
(00120)	SF SW-9 "2432", scheme #2, *97*	199.95	_____
(00121)	UP SW-9 "1841", scheme #1, *97*	199.95	_____
(00122)	UP SW-9 "1862", scheme #2, *97*	199.95	_____
(00123)	UP Stock Car, scheme #3, *97*	39.95	_____
(00124)	Unlettered Rebuilt, red, *97*	39.95	_____
(00125)	C&O Rebuilt "12681", *97*	39.95	_____
(00126)	CNW Rebuilt, *97*	39.95	_____
(00127)	DL&W Rebuilt "48001", *97*	39.95	_____
(00128)	Frisco Rebuilt "128011", *97*	39.95	_____
(00129)	NYC Rebuilt, *97*	39.95	_____
(00130)	NYC/PMKY Rebuilt "83401", *97*	39.95	_____
(00131)	PRR #1 Rebuilt, *97*	39.95	_____
(00132)	PRR #2 Rebuilt, *97*	39.95	_____
(00133)	SF #1 Rebuilt, *97*	39.95	_____
(00134)	SF #2 Rebuilt, *97*	39.95	_____
(00135)	VC Rebuilt, *97*	39.95	_____
(00136)	CN Stock Car "810522", *97*	39.95	_____
(00137)	CB&Q Stock Car "52881", *97*	39.95	_____
(00138)	MP Stock Car "154092", *97*	39.95	_____
(00139)	MKT Stock Car "47021", *97*	39.95	_____
(00140)	UP Stock Car "0SL39193", *97*	39.95	_____
(00141)	Rutland USRA Wooden Boxcar, *97*	39.95	_____
(00142)	Clinchfield USRA Wooden Boxcar "8051", *97*	39.95	_____
(00143)	Erie USRA Wooden Boxcar, *97*	39.95	_____
(00144)	MILW USRA Wooden Boxcar, *97*	39.95	_____

(00145)	PRR-MOW USRA Wooden Boxcar, *97*	39.95	_____
(00146)	SF USRA Wooden Boxcar, *97*	39.95	_____
(00147)	Wabash USRA Wooden Boxcar, *97*	39.95	_____
(00148)	Chessie/B&O SW-9 Diesel Switcher "B&O 9602", *97–98*	199.95	_____
(00149)	CN 40' Stock Car "810371", *97–98*	39.95	_____
(00150)	CB&Q 40' Stock Car "52251", *97–98*	39.95	_____
(00151)	MKT 40' Stock Car "47372", *97–98*	39.95	_____
(00152)	UP/OSL 40' Stock Car "39341", scheme #2, *97–98*	39.95	_____
(00153)	C&O 40' Rebuilt Steel Boxcar "12684", *97*	39.95	_____
(00154)	Frisco 40' Rebuilt Steel Boxcar "128000", *97*	39.95	_____
(00155)	Unlettered 53'6" Bulkhead Flatcar, *97–98*	49.95	_____
(00156)	BN 53'6" Bulkhead Flatcar "629091", scheme #1, *97–98*	49.95	_____
(00157)	BN 53'6" Bulkhead Flatcar "629052", scheme #2, *97–98*	49.95	_____
(00158)	CB&Q 53'6" Bulkhead Flatcar "95221", scheme #2, *97–98*	49.95	_____
(00159)	CB&Q 53'6" Bulkhead Flatcar "95282", scheme #1, *97–98*	49.95	_____
(00160)	D&RGW 53'6" Bulkhead Flatcar "22761", *97–98*	49.95	_____
(00161)	IC 53'6" Bulkhead Flatcar "92641", scheme #1, *97–98*	49.95	_____
(00162)	IC 53'6" Bulkhead Flatcar "92642", scheme #2, *97–98*	49.95	_____
(00163)	SOU 53'6" Bulkhead Flatcar "51861", *97–98*	49.95	_____
(00164)	UP 53'6" Bulkhead Flatcar "15061", scheme #1, *97–98*	49.95	_____
(00165)	UP 53'6" Bulkhead Flatcar "15082", scheme #2, *97–98*	49.95	_____
(00166)	Wabash 53'6" Bulkhead Flatcar "181", *97–98*	49.95	_____
(00167)	Unlettered 53'6" Standard Flatcar, *97–98*	39.95	_____
(00168)	Unlettered 53'6" Standard Flatcar, *97–98*	39.95	_____
(00169)	BN 53'6" Standard Flatcar "629091", *97–98*	39.95	_____
(00170)	CB&Q 53'6" Standard Flatcar "95221", *97–98*	39.95	_____
(00171)	D&RGW 53'6" Standard Flatcar "22761", *97–98*	39.95	_____
(00172)	IC 53'6" Standard Flatcar "92641", *97–98*	39.95	_____
(00173)	SOU 53'6" Standard Flatcar "51861", *97–98*	39.95	_____
(00174)	UP 53'6" Standard Flatcar "15061", *97–98*	39.95	_____
(00175)	Wabash 53'6" Standard Flatcar "181", *97–98*	39.95	_____

		Retail	Cond/$
(00176)	PRR 53'6" Standard Flatcar "469997", *97–98*	39.95	_____
(00177)	Unlettered 53'6" Trailer on Flatcar, *97–98*	59.95	_____
(00178)	B&A 53'6" Trailer on Flatcar "451", *97–98*	59.95	_____
(00179)	NKP 53'6" Trailer on Flatcar "3021", *97–98*	59.95	_____
(00180)	RI 53'6" Trailer on Flatcar "90991", *97–98*	59.95	_____
(00181)	PRR 53'6" Trailer on Flatcar "92761", scheme #1, *97–98*	59.95	_____
(00182)	PRR 53'6" Trailer on Flatcar "92762", scheme #2, *97–98*	59.95	_____
(00183)	Seaboard 53'6" Trailer on Flatcar "47101", *97–98*	59.95	_____
(00184)	UP 53'6" Trailer on Flatcar "15321", scheme #1, *97–98*	59.95	_____
(00185)	UP 53'6" Trailer on Flatcar "15322", scheme #2, *97–98*	59.95	_____
(00186)	Unlettered 53'6" Trailer on Flatcar, *97–98*	59.95	_____
(00187)	C&NW 53'6" Trailer on Flatcar "44151", *97–98*	59.95	_____
(00188)	C&NW 53'6" Trailer on Flatcar "44152", *97–98*	59.95	_____
(00189)	NH 53'6" Trailer on Flatcar "17341", scheme #1, *97–98*	59.95	_____
(00190)	NH 53'6" Trailer on Flatcar "17382", scheme #2, *97–98*	59.95	_____
(00191)	NYC 53'6" Trailer on Flatcar "499701", scheme #1, *97–98*	59.95	_____
(00192)	NYC 53'6" Trailer on Flatcar "499612", scheme #2, *97–98*	59.95	_____
(00193)	TTX/REAX 53'6" Trailer on Flatcar "475001", *97–98*	59.95	_____
(00194)	TTX/REAX 53'6" Trailer on Flatcar "475002", *97–98*	59.95	_____
(00195)	Unlettered 35' Horizontal Corr. Trailer, *97–98*	15.95	_____
(00196)	Unlettered 35' Vertical Post Trailer, *97–98*	15.95	_____
(00197)	B&A 35' Horizontal Corr. Trailer, *97–98*	15.95	_____
(00198)	NKP 35' Horizontal Corr. Trailer, *97–98*	15.95	_____
(00199)	RI 35' Horizontal Corr. Trailer, *97–98*	15.95	_____
(00200)	PRR 35' Horizontal Corr. Trailer, *97–98*	15.95	_____
(00201)	Seaboard 35' Horizontal Corr. Trailer, *97–98*	15.95	_____
(00202)	UP 35' Horizontal Corr. Trailer, *97–98*	15.95	_____
(00203)	C&NW 35' Vertical Post Trailer, *97–98*	15.95	_____
(00204)	NH 35' Vertical Post Trailer, *97–98*	15.95	_____
(00205)	NYC 35' Vertical Post Trailer, *97–98*	15.95	_____

		Retail	Cond/$
(00206)	REA 35' Vertical Post Trailer, scheme #1, *97–98*	15.95	_____
(00207)	REA 35' Vertical Post Trailer, scheme #2, *97–98*	15.95	_____
(00208)	B&A 53'6" Standard Flatcar "451", *97–98*	39.95	_____
(00209)	C&NW 53'6" Standard Flatcar "44151", *97–98*	39.95	_____
(00210)	NH 53'6" Standard Flatcar "17341", *97–98*	39.95	_____
(00211)	NYC 53'6" Standard Flatcar "499701", *97–98*	39.95	_____
(00212)	NKP 53'6" Standard Flatcar "3021", *97–98*	39.95	_____
(00213)	PRR 53'6" Standard Flatcar "92761", *97–98*	39.95	_____
(00214)	RI 53'6" Standard Flatcar "90991", *97–98*	39.95	_____
(00215)	Seaboard 53'6" Standard Flatcar "47101", *97–98*	39.95	_____
(00216)	UP 53'6" Standard Flatcar "15321", *97–98*	39.95	_____
(00217)	Unlettered Wide Vision Caboose, *98*	69.95	_____
(00218)	BN Wide Vision Caboose, scheme #1, *98*	69.95	_____
(00219)	BN Wide Vision Caboose, scheme #2, *98*	69.95	_____
(00220)	C&O Wide Vision Caboose, scheme #1, *98*	69.95	_____
(00221)	C&O Wide Vision Caboose, scheme #2, *98*	69.95	_____
(00222)	CB&Q Wide Vision Caboose, scheme #1, *98*	69.95	_____
(00223)	CB&Q Wide Vision Caboose, scheme #2, *98*	69.95	_____
(00224)	CSX Wide Vision Caboose, scheme #1, *98*	69.95	_____
(00225)	CSX Wide Vision Caboose, scheme #2, *98*	69.95	_____
(00226)	C&NW Wide Vision Caboose, scheme #1, *98*	69.95	_____
(00227)	C&NW Wide Vision Caboose, scheme #2, *98*	69.95	_____
(00228)	Conrail Wide Vision Caboose, scheme #1, *98*	69.95	_____
(00229)	Conrail Wide Vision Caboose, scheme #2, *98*	69.95	_____
(00230)	D&RGW Wide Vision Caboose, scheme #1, *98*	69.95	_____
(00231)	D&RGW Wide Vision Caboose, scheme #1, *98*	69.95	_____
(00232)	GN Wide Vision Caboose, scheme #1, *98*	69.95	_____
(00233)	GN Wide Vision Caboose, scheme #2, *98*	69.95	_____
(00234)	IC Wide Vision Caboose, scheme #1, *98*	69.95	_____
(00235)	IC Wide Vision Caboose, scheme #2, *98*	69.95	_____
(00236)	MP Wide Vision Caboose, scheme #1, *98*	69.95	_____
(00237)	MP Wide Vision Caboose, scheme #2, *98*	69.95	_____
(00238)	NP Wide Vision Caboose, scheme #1, *98*	69.95	_____
(00239)	NP Wide Vision Caboose, scheme #2, *98*	69.95	_____
(00240)	AT&SF Wide Vision Caboose, scheme #1, *98*	69.95	_____
(00241)	AT&SF Wide Vision Caboose, scheme #2, *98*	69.95	_____

		Retail	Cond/$
(00242)	Seaboard Wide Vision Caboose, scheme #1, *98*	69.95	_____
(00243)	Seaboard Wide Vision Caboose, scheme #2, *98*	69.95	_____
(00244)	SOO Line Wide Vision Caboose, scheme #1, *98*	69.95	_____
(00245)	SOO Line Wide Vision Caboose, scheme #2, *98*	69.95	_____
(00246)	Evans Building Materials Load, *97–98*	9.95	_____
(00247)	Gold Bond Building Material Load, white, *97–98*	9.95	_____
(00248)	Gold Bond Building Material Load, red, *97–98*	9.95	_____
(00249)	Johns Manville Building Material Load, *97–98*	9.95	_____
(00250)	Masonite Building Material Load, *97–98*	9.95	_____
(00251)	Plumb Creek Building Material Load, *97–98*	9.95	_____
(00252)	United States Gypsum Building Material Load, *97–98*	9.95	_____
(00253)	155# Rail Joiner/Connector, 12/pkg, *98*	4.95	_____
(00254)	155# Rail Insulated Joiner/Connector, 12/pkg, *98*	2.95	_____
(00255)	155# Rail Joiner/Connector w/ feeder wire, 12/pkg, *98*	7.95	_____
(00256)	155# NS Track Set, 20" radius, 16 pieces, *98*	69.95	_____
(00257)	155# NS 15" Straight Track, 6/box, *98*	36.95	_____
(00258)	155# NS 10" Straight Track, 6/box, *98*	29.95	_____
(00259)	155# NS Curved Track, 20" radius, 30°, 6/box, *98*	29.95	_____
(00260)	BN 53'6" Standard Flatcar "629052", scheme #2, *97–98*	39.95	_____
(00261)	UP 53'6" Standard Flatcar "15082", scheme #2, *97–98*	39.95	_____
(00262)	B&M 53'6" Trailer on Flatcar, "5205", 1998 NASG Conv. Car, *98*	59.95	_____
(00263)	B&M 53'6" Standard Flatcar, "5202", *98*	39.95	_____
(00264)	B&M 35' Vert. Post Trailer, "150", 1998 NASG Conv. Car, *98*	15.95	_____
(00265)	36" Scale Wheelsets 4/Pack, *94–99*	3.95	_____
(00266)	Milwaukee Road #1 Wide Vision Caboose, "992301", *98*	69.95	_____
(00267)	Milwaukee Road #2 Wide Vision Caboose, "992302", *98*	69.95	_____

		Retail	Cond/$
(00268)	MEC Wide Vision Caboose, "671", 1998 Christmas Cab, *98*	69.95	_____
(00269)	Montana Rail Link #1 Wide Vision Caboose, *N/A*	69.95	_____
(00270)	Montana Rail Link #2 Wide Vision Caboose, *N/A*	69.95	_____
(00271)	Unlettered-FB 3-bay Covered Hopper, *99*	39.95	_____
(00272)	AT&SF (GA-90) 3-bay Covered Hopper, "300171", *99*	39.95	_____
(00273)	BN 3-bay Covered Hopper, *99*	39.95	_____
(00274)	Chessie 3-bay Covered Hopper, "B&O 628031", *99*	39.95	_____
(00275)	CB&Q 3-bay Covered Hopper, "85021", *99*	39.95	_____
(00276)	C&NW 3-bay Covered Hopper, "435041", *99*	39.95	_____
(00277)	Conrail 3-bay Covered Hopper, "883581", *99*	39.95	_____
(00278)	GN 3-bay Covered Hopper, "71971", *99*	39.95	_____
(00279)	Erie Lackawanna 3-bay Covered Hopper, "21801", *99*	39.95	_____
(00280)	NYC 3-bay Covered Hopper, "883051", *99*	39.95	_____
(00281)	UP 3-bay Covered Hopper, "1921", *99*	39.95	_____
(00282)	C&NW/MStL (2) 2-bay Covered Hopper, *99*	39.95	_____
(00283)	Jack Frost 2-bay Covered Hopper, *99*	39.95	_____
(00284)	LNE 2-bay Covered Hopper, "18101-200", *99*	39.95	_____
(00285)	MStL (NASG) 2-bay Covered Hopper, "70401-599", *99*	39.95	_____
(00286)	CSX (Central Soya) 2-bay Covered Hopper, "145-159", *99*	39.95	_____
(00287)	NAHX (poly-borate) #1, 2-bay Covered Hopper, "31067", *99*	39.95	_____
(00288)	NAHX (poly-borate) #2, 2-bay Covered Hopper, "31067", *99*	39.95	_____
(00289)	Engineer & Fireman, Painted Seated Figures, *98*	5.95	_____
(00290)	AC/DC Rev Unit w/DCC SOC Diesel Part, *98*	250	_____
(00291)	S-19 Radius 15° Curved Track, 6/box, *98*	26.95	_____
(00292)	S-24 Radius 30° Curved Track, 6/box, *99*	34.95	_____
(00293)	S-24 Radius 15° Curved Track, 6/box, *99*	27.95	_____

		Retail	Cond/$
(00294)	S-29 Radius 30° Curved Track, 6/box, *99*	36.95	_____
(00295)	SW-9 coupler, AF-compatible, pair, *98*	3.95	_____
(00296)	S-29 Radius 15° Curved Track, 6/box, *99*	29.95	_____
(00297)	5" Straight Track 6/box Track, *99*	24.95	_____
(00298)	RC Switches #3 RH Track, *N/A*		
(00299)	RC Switches #3 LH Track, *N/A*		
(00300)	AT&SF 53'6" Trailer on Flatcar, "92752", *98*	59.95	_____
(00301)	B&O 53'6" Trailer on Flatcar, "8742", *98*	59.95	_____
(00302)	Maine Central 53'6" Bulkhead Flatcar, "7712", *99*	49.95	_____
(00303)	CP/Speedway 53'6" Trailer on Flatcar, "505012", *98*	59.95	_____
(00304)	GN 53'6" Trailer on Flatcar, "60242", *98*	59.95	_____
(00305)	NH/Yale 53'6" Trailer on Flatcar, "17343", *98*	59.95	_____
(00306)	PRR 53'6" Trailer on Flatcar, "92763", *98*	59.95	_____
(00307)	TTX/Carolina 53'6" Trailer on Flatcar, "475083", *98*	59.95	_____
(00308)	Rio Grande 53'6" Trailer on Flatcar, "500002", *98*	59.95	_____
(00309)	UP 53'6" Standard Flatcar w/excavator, "58073", *98*	39.95	_____
(00310)	WM 53'6" Trailer on Flatcar, "7002", *98*	59.95	_____
(00311)	AT&SF 53'6" Standard Flatcar, "92752", *98*	39.95	_____
(00312)	B&O 53'6" Standard Flatcar, "8742", *99*	39.95	_____
(00313)	Maine Central 53'6" Standard Flatcar, "7712", *99*	39.95	_____
(00314)	CP 53'6" Standard Flatcar, "505012", *98*	39.95	_____
(00315)	GN 53'6" Standard Flatcar, "60062", *98*	39.95	_____
(00316)	NH #3 53'6" Standard Flatcar, "17343", *98*	39.95	_____
(00317)	PRR #3 53'6" Standard Flatcar, "92763", *98*	39.95	_____
(00318)	D&RGW 53'6" Standard Flatcar, "500002", *98*	39.95	_____
(00319)	UP #4 53'6" Standard Flatcar, *N/A*	39.95	_____
(00320)	WM 53'6" Standard Flatcar, "7002", *98*	39.95	_____
(00321)	AT&SF 35' Horizontal Corr. Trailer, *98*	15.95	_____
(00322)	B&O 35' Horizontal Corr. Trailer, *99*	15.95	_____
(00323)	Speedway 35' Horizontal Corr. Trailer, *98*	15.95	_____
(00324)	GN 35' Horizontal Corr. Trailer, "G322", *98*	15.95	_____
(00325)	Yale 35' Vert. Post Trailer, *98*	15.95	_____

		Retail	Cond/$
(00326)	PRR 35' Vert. Post Trailer, *98*	15.95	_____
(00327)	Carolina 35' Vert. Post Trailer, *98*	15.95	_____
(00328)	D&RGW 35' Horizontal Post Trailer, *98*	15.95	_____
(00329)	UP #2 35' Horizontal Corr. Trailer, *N/A*	15.95	_____
(00330)	WM 35' Vert. Post Trailer, *98*	15.95	_____
(00331)	AT&SF #1 53'6" Bulkhead Flatcar, *98*	49.95	_____
(00332)	AT&SF #2 53'6" Bulkhead Flatcar, *98*	49.95	_____
(00333)	GN #1 53'6" Bulkhead Flatcar, "60342", *98*	49.95	_____
(00334)	GN #2 53'6" Bulkhead Flatcar, "60403", *98*	49.95	_____
(00335)	Soo Line #1 53'6" Bulkhead Flatcar, "5573", *98*	49.95	_____
(00336)	Soo Line #2 53'6" Bulkhead Flatcar, *98*	49.95	_____
(00337)	D&H 53'6" Bulkhead Flatcar "16502", *97–98*	49.95	_____
(00338)	WM/Chessie 53'6" Bulkhead Flatcar "WM 402", *97–98*	39.95	_____
(00339)	Santa Fe #2 53'6" Standard Flatcar, *97–98*	39.95	_____
(00340)	Great Northern #2 53'6" Standard Flatcar, "60403", *97–98*	39.95	_____
(00341)	Soo Line #2 53'6" Standard Flatcar, "5573", *97–98*	39.95	_____
(00342)	Delaware & Hudson 53'6" Standard Flatcar, "16502", *97–98*	39.95	_____
(00343)	WM/Chessie 53'6" Standard Flatcar, "WM 402", *97–98*	39.95	_____
(00344)	Santa Fe 3-car set, *97–98*	99.95	_____
(00345)	C&NW 3-car set, *97–98*	99.95	_____
(00346)	GN #1 40' Rebuilt Steel Boxcar, "27001", *97–98*	39.95	_____
(00347)	GN #2 40' Rebuilt Steel Boxcar, "27792", *97–98*	39.95	_____
(00348)	MoPac #2 40' Rebuilt Steel Boxcar, *99*	39.95	_____
(00349)	MoPac #1 40' Rebuilt Steel Boxcar, *99*	39.95	_____
(00350)	NYC 3-car set, *99*	99.95	_____
(00351)	RS&P 40' Rebuilt Steel Boxcar, *99*	39.95	_____
(00352)	UP 3-car set, *99*	99.95	_____
(00353)	Ball Lines 40' Rebuilt Steel Boxcar, *99*	39.95	_____
(00354)	Gear Box, AF Comp Drivers, *98*	9.95	_____
(00355)	Gear Box, code 110 Drivers, *98*	9.95	_____
(00356)	DCC Socket/DC Plug/AC pcb, *98*	39.95	_____
(00357)	SW-9 Coupler, AF-compatible, bulk, *98*	3.95	_____
(00358)	Conductor and Brakeman, Painted Figures (Seated), *98*	5.95	_____

		Retail	Cond/$
(00359)	EVC Coupler, AF compatible, pair, *98*	2.95	_____
(00360)	10" Straight Track, Steel Rail, Bulk, *N/A*	—	_____
(00361)	S-19, 30" Straight Track, Steel Rail, Bulk, *N/A*	—	_____
(00362)	B&O #1, Diesel Cab, A&B set, "82", *99*	499.95	_____
(00363)	B&O #2, Diesel Cab, A&B set, "84", *99*	499.95	_____
(00364)	CB&Q #1, Diesel Cab, A&B set, "161", *99*	499.95	_____
(00365)	CB&Q #2, Diesel Cab, A&B set, "162", *99*	499.95	_____
(00366)	C&NW #1, Diesel Cab, A&B set, "201", *99*	499.95	_____
(00367)	C&NW #2, Diesel Cab, A&B set, "201", *99*	499.95	_____
(00368)	DL&W #1, Diesel Cab, A&B set, "803A-B", *99*	499.95	_____
(00369)	DL&W #2, Diesel Cab, A&B set, "805A-B", *99*	499.95	_____
(00370)	Maine Central #1, Diesel Cab, A&B set, "671", *99*	499.95	_____
(00371)	Maine Central #2, Diesel Cab, A&B set, "672", *99*	499.95	_____
(00372)	NYC #1, Diesel Cab, A&B set, "3501", *99*	499.95	_____
(00373)	NYC #2, Diesel Cab, A&B set, "3502", *99*	499.95	_____
(00374)	Southern #1, Diesel Cab, A&B set, "4171/4353", *99*	499.95	_____
(00375)	Southern #2, Diesel Cab, A&B set, "4172/4354", *99*	499.95	_____
(00376)	SP #1, Diesel Cab, A&B set, "6100s", *99*	499.95	_____
(00377)	SP #2, Diesel Cab, A&B set, "6100s", *99*	499.95	_____
(00378)	UP #1, Diesel Cab, A&B set, "1400s", *99*	499.95	_____
(00379)	UP #2, Diesel Cab, A&B set, "1400s", *99*	499.95	_____
(00380)	WP #1, Diesel Cab, A&B set, "801", *99*	499.95	_____
(00381)	WP #2, Diesel Cab, A&B set, "802", *99*	499.95	_____
(00382)	Undecorated, Diesel Cab, A&B set, *99*	499.95	_____
(00383)	Barber EVC, RB code 110 Truck, *98*	9.95	_____
(00384)	Barber EVC, RB AF-compatible Truck, *98*	9.95	_____
(00385)	NYC Frt. #1, Diesel Cab, A&B set, "1600s", *99*	499.95	_____
(00386)	NYC Frt. #2, Diesel Cab, A&B set, "1600s", *99*	499.95	_____
(00387)	UP, NMRA 1998 Convention Car, "15322", *98*	59.95	_____
(00388)	Boise Cascade Wrapped Lumber Load, *98*	14.95	_____
(00389)	Finlay Premium Wrapped Lumber Load, *98*	14.95	_____
(00390)	Western Carrier Wrapped Lumber Load, *98*	14.95	_____
(00391)	Weyerhaeuser Wrapped Lumber Load, *98*	14.95	_____

		Retail	Cond/$
(00392)	Pulpwood Load, *98*	14.95	_____
(00393)	AF Track Adaptor, 8/pkg, *00*	CP	_____
(00394)	Bulb, 2.5-volt EVC 2/pkg, *00*	CP	_____
(00395)	Rail Joiner, insulated, yel. 12/pkg , *00*	CP	_____
(00396)	AT&SF #2 PS-2 3-bay "300142", *00*	39.95	_____
(00397)	Burlington Northern #2 PS-2 3-bay "435409", *00*	39.95	_____
(00398)	Chessie #2 PS-2 3-bay B&O "628182", *00*	39.95	_____
(00399)	CB&Q #2 PS-2 3-bay "85121", *00*	39.95	_____
(00400)	Chicago Northwestern #2 PS-2 3-bay "95432", *00*	39.95	_____
(00401)	Conrail #2 PS-2 3-bay "883672", *00*	39.95	_____
(00402)	GN #2 PS-2 3-bay "71971", *00*	39.95	_____
(00403)	Erie Lackawanna #2 PS-2 3-bay "21892", *00*	39.95	_____
(00404)	New York Central #2 PS-2 3-bay "883092", *00*	39.95	_____
(00405)	Union Pacific #2 PS-2 3-bay "19192", *00*	39.95	_____
(00406)	Constant Lighting, 2.5-volt elec., *00*	CP	_____
(00407)	CNW/M&StL #2 PS-2, *00*	39.95	_____
(00408)	LNE #2 PS-2 "18224", *00*	39.95	_____
(00409)	Central Soya (CSX) #2 PS-2 "145", *00*	39.95	_____
(00410)	Roscoe, Snyder & Pacific #2 RBLT "32", *00*	39.95	_____
(00411)	Ball Lines #2 RBLT "1424", *00*	39.95	_____
(00412)	CB&Q (black) #1 PS-2 3-bay "85000", *00*	39.95	_____
(00413)	Jack Frost #2 PS-2 "331", *00*	39.95	_____
(00414)	Cedar Heights Clay PS-2 "111", *00*	39.95	_____
(00415)	Ann Arbor #1(TCA) PS-2 "781", *00*	39.95	_____
(00416)	Ann Arbor #2(TCA) PS-2 "789", *00*	39.95	_____
(00417)	M&StL #1 (NASG) PS-2 3-bay "71001", *00*	39.95	_____
(00418)	M&StL #2 (NASG) PS-2 3-bay "71033", *00*	39.95	_____
(00419)	M&StL #2 (NASG) PS-2 "70525", *00*	39.95	_____
(00420)	CB&Q (black) #2 PS-2 3-bay "85011", *00*	39.95	_____
(00421)	Conrail SW-9 set, *00*	CP	_____
(00422)	BN SW-9 set. *00*	CP	_____
(00423)	AT&SF SW-9 6 car set set, *00*	CP	_____
(00424)	Chessie SW-9 set, *00*	CP	_____
(00425)	NMRA 1999 Comm. Car USRA GSV "2084", *00*	59.95	_____
(00426)	Chesapeake & Ohio #1 SW-9 "5093", *00*	199.95	_____
(00427)	Chesapeake & Ohio #2 SW-9 "5084", *00*	199.95	_____
(00428)	Great Northern #1 SW-9 "15", *00*	199.95	_____
(00429)	Great Northern #2 SW-9 "14", *00*	199.95	_____
(00430)	D&RGW #1 SW-9 "133", *00*	199.95	_____
(00431)	D&RGW #2 SW-9 "134", *00*	199.95	_____
(00432)	ICG #1 SW-9 "1223", *00*	199.95	_____

		Retail	Cond/$
(00433)	ICG #2 SW-9 "1234", *00*	199.95	_____
(00434)	Northern Pacific #1 SW-9 "133", *00*	199.95	_____
(00435)	Northern Pacific #2 SW-9 "133", *00*	199.95	_____
(00436)	UP (2nd sch) #1 SW-9 "1833", *00*	199.95	_____
(00437)	UP (2nd sch) #2 SW-9 "1854", *00*	199.95	_____
(00438)	Unlettered SW-1, *00*	CP	_____
(00439)	Boston & Maine #1 SW-1 "1113", *00*	CP	_____
(00440)	Boston & Maine #2 SW-1 "1114", *00*	CP	_____
(00441)	Chessie System #1 SW-1 B&O "8403", *00*	CP	_____
(00442)	Chessie System #2 SW-1 B&O "8414", *00*	CP	_____
(00443)	C&NW #1 SW-1 "1213", *00*	CP	_____
(00444)	C&NW #2 SW-1 "1214", *00*	CP	_____
(00445)	WP #1 SW-1 "5103", *00*	CP	_____
(00446)	WP #2 SW-1 "5104", *00*	CP	_____
(00447)	Milwaukee Road #1 SW-1 "1613", *00*	CP	_____
(00448)	Milwaukee Road #2 SW-1 "1634", *00*	CP	_____
(00449)	PRR #1 SW-1 "5953", *00*	CP	_____
(00450)	PRR #2 SW-1 "5944", *00*	CP	_____
(00451)	Seaboard SW-1 "1200", *00*	CP	_____
(00452)	Soo Line SW-1 "320", *00*	CP	_____
(00453)	Lehigh Valley #1 SW-1, *00*	CP	_____
(00454)	Lehigh Valley #2 SW-1, *00*	CP	_____
(00455)	SP #1 SW-1 "1013", *00*	CP	_____
(00456)	SP #2 SW-1 "1004", *00*	CP	_____
(00457)	C&O SW-9 set, *00*	CP	_____
(00458)	Conrail SW-9 set, *00*	CP	_____
(00459)	D&RGW SW-9 set, *00*	CP	_____
(00460)	GN SW-9 set, *00*	CP	_____
(00461)	ICG SW-9 set, *00*	CP	_____
(00462)	NP SW-9 set, *00*	CP	_____

GILBERT PAPER
1946–1966

1946

D1451	Consumer Catalog			
	(A) As above	35	125	_____
	(B) w/ red binder	50	255	_____
No number	Envelope for D1451	3	8	_____
D1455	Dealer Catalog	30	110	_____
D1457	Gilbert Scientific Toys	10	20	_____
D1458	Appointment Card	0.50	1.50	_____
M2499	Instruction Sheet	0.25	1	_____

1947

D1462	Catalog Mailer	15	65	_____
D1472	Catalog Mailer	15	65	_____
D1473	Consumer Catalog	25	80	_____
No number	Envelope for D1473	3	5	_____
D1482	Dealer Catalog	20	49	_____
D1492	Erector Fun and Action	5	15	_____
D1495	What Retail Stores Should Know	5	15	_____
D1496	Display Suggestions	50	300	_____
D1502	Advance Catalog	12	35	_____
M2502	Instruction Book	2	4	_____

1948

D1505	Advance Catalog	10	34	_____
D1507	Consumer Catalog	15	75	_____
D1508	Superman	15	65	_____
D1508	Consumer Catalog			
	(A) As above	10	26	_____
	(B) Postage Prepaid	5	20	_____
D1517	HO Catalog	10	25	_____

1949

D1524	Gilbert Scientific Toys Catalog	5	10	_____
D1525	Bang Bang Torpedo	50	100	_____
D1530	Advance Catalog	20	46	_____
D1531	Gilbert Scientific Toys Catalog	5	10	_____
D1535	Consumer Catalog		NRS	_____
D1536	Consumer Catalog	10	50	_____
D1547	Catalog Envelope	2	5	_____
D1552	How to Sell American Flyer	5	20	_____
M2690	Instruction Booklet			
	(A) Yellow cover	2	5	_____
	(B) White cover	4	10	_____

1950

D1578	Dealer Catalog	12	55	_____
D1579	Gilbert Toys	6	16	_____
D1581/D1581A	Red/blue Ad		NRS	_____
D1604	Consumer Catalog	15	49	_____
D1610	Catalog Envelope	2	5	_____

		Good	Exc	Cond/$
D1629	Dealer Action Displays Sheet		NRS	_____
D1631	Dealer TV Ad	10	20	_____
No number	Ready Again Booklet		NRS	_____
	1951			
D1637	Dealer Catalog	10	25	_____
D1637A	Advance Catalog	8	25	_____
D1640	Consumer Catalog	15	50	_____
D1641	Erector and Gilbert Toys Catalog	3	6	_____
D1652	Facts About AF Trains		NRS	_____
D1656	AF and Toys	5	10	_____
D1660	Gilbert Electric Eye	5	10	_____
	1952			
D1667	Advance Catalog	10	40	_____
D1667A	Advance Catalog	10	30	_____
D1668A	Consumer Catalog		NRS	_____
D1670	Single Sheet 200 Series Bldgs.	3	10	_____
D1677	Consumer Catalog	10	41	_____
D1678	Facts About AF Trains	8	12	_____
M2978	AF Model Railroad Handbook	6	11	_____
M2984	Instruction Book	1	4	_____
No number	Advance Catalog		NRS	_____
No Number	Consumer Catalog, Spanish		NRS	_____
	1953			
D1699	Consumer Catalog		NRS	_____
D1703	Erector and Other Toys	3	6	_____
D1704	Dealer Catalog	8	35	_____
D1714	Dealer Catalog, East	8	22	_____
D1715	Consumer Catalog, West	10	31	_____
D1727	Tips on Selling AF Trains	5	10	_____
D1728	Tips on Erector	3	9	_____
	1954			
D1734	Catalog Envelope	2	5	_____
D1740	Erector and Gilbert Toys	1	5	_____
D1744	AF and Erector Ad Program	5	18	_____
D1746	Dealer Catalog			
	(A) Pulp	8	20	_____
	(B) Glossy	8	25	_____
D1748	Catalog, East			
	(A) Consumer	3	11	_____
	(B) Dealer	5	16	_____
D1749	Dealer Catalog, West	10	25	_____
D1750	Dealer Displays		NRS	_____
D1751	Microscope Flysheet	1	3	_____
D1760	Consumer Catalog, East	10	36	_____
D1761	Consumer Catalog, West	10	30	_____
D1762	Boys RR Club Letter	2	5	_____

		Good	Exc	Cond/$
D1769	Read All About Ad Campaign		NRS	_____
D1774	Erector and Other Gilbert Toys	3	6	_____
D1777	Reply Postcard	1	3	_____
M3290	Instruction Book	2	5	_____
	1955			
D1782	Dealer Catalog	6	18	_____
D1783	Certificate of Registry	5	10	_____
D1784	Erector and Other Gilbert Toys		NRS	_____
D1801	Consumer Catalog, East	5	21	_____
D1802	Consumer Catalog, West	8	20	_____
D1814	Choo Choo Sound Foldout	1	5	_____
D1816	Dealer Catalog	10	25	_____
D1820	HO Consumer Catalog	1	3	_____
D1835	Tips for Selling Erector	1	3	_____
D1840	Envelope	1	5	_____
M3450	Instruction Book	1	4	_____
	1956			
D1866	Consumer Catalog, East	6	26	_____
D1867	Consumer Catalog, West	10	31	_____
D1874	Dealer Catalog	15	40	_____
D1879	Gilbert and Erector Toys	1	7	_____
D1882	AF and Erector Displays	1	7	_____
D1899	Big Value American Flyer Railroad Trestle System Special Set Brochure		NRS	_____
D1904	Gilbert HO Catalog	2	12	_____
D1907	Dealer Catalog	6	25	_____
D1920	How to Build a Model Railroad	2	10	_____
D1922	Miniature Catalog	6	25	_____
D1925	Erector Folder	2	8	_____
D1926	Envelope for D1922 Catalog	2	5	_____
	1957			
D1937	Dealer Catalog	7	15	_____
D1966	Consumer Catalog	2	8	_____
D1973	Erector and Other Toys	1	3	_____
D1980	Cardboard		NRS	_____
D1981	Same as D1980		NRS	_____
D2006	Consumer Catalog, East	5	21	_____
D2007	Consumer Catalog, West	12	30	_____
D2008	Erector and Toys	1	5	_____
D2022	Dealer Flyer		NRS	_____
D2031	Consumer Catalog		NRS	_____
D2037	Erector and Gilbert Toys	1	6	_____
D2045	Gilbert Promotion Kit		NRS	_____
M3817	HO Instructions	2	8	_____
No number	Same as M3450 (1955) but w/o number		NRS	_____

		Good	Exc	Cond/$
	1958			
D2047	Consumer Catalog	20	85	_____
D2048	Catalog, West	25	70	_____
D2058	Erector and Toys	1	5	_____
D2060	Erector and Gilbert Toys	2	10	_____
D2073	Advance Catalog	5	15	_____
D2080	Smoking Caboose		NRS	_____
D2086	Consumer Folder, East	3	15	_____
D2087	Consumer Folder, West	1	10	_____
D2088	Consumer Folder	3	15	_____
D2101	Career Building Science Toys	1	3	_____
D4106	HO Catalog	2	5	_____
M4195	Accessory Folder	1	5	_____
M4202	Color Billboards		NRS	_____
	1959			
D2115	Dealer Catalog	12	35	_____
No Number	Canadian, D2115		NRS	_____
D2118	AF No. 20142, Willit		NRS	_____
D2120	Career Building Science Toys	1	5	_____
D2125	Overland Express Sheet	1	3	_____
D2146	Consumer Catalog	1	5	_____
D2148	Consumer Catalog	1	5	_____
D2171-D2179	Dealer Promotional Set		NRS	_____
D2179	Promotional Sheet, Franklin Set	1	5	_____
D2180	Gilbert Science Toys	1	5	_____
No Number	Catalog, Gilbert Toys		NRS	_____
M4225	Train Assembly and Operating Instructions		—	_____
M4326	Accessory Catalog	1	5	_____
M4869	AF Maintenance Manual	1	3	_____
	1960			
D2192	Catalog			
	(A) Dealer	6	15	_____
	(B) Advance		1	_____
D2193	Consumer Catalog	2	8	_____
D2193REV	Revised Consumer Catalog	2	8	_____
D2198	Action and Fun Catalog	3	7	_____
D2205	Gilbert Toys	2	4	_____
D2208	Dealer Advance Catalog		NRS	_____
D2223	Gilbert Science Toys	1	4	_____
D2224	Consumer Folder	2	6	_____
D2225	Consumer Folder	3	6	_____
D2226	Consumer Folder	2	5	_____
D2230	Consumer Catalog	9	40	_____
D2231	Consumer Catalog	3	10	_____
No Number	Promotional Sheet, Truscott Set		NRS	_____

		Good	Exc	Cond/$
1961				
D2238	Career Building Science Toys	3	15	_____
D2239	Consumer Catalog	5	18	_____
D2242REV	Auto Rama Catalog	0.50	2	_____
D2255	1961–62 Retail Display	0.50	2	_____
D2266	Gilbert Science Toys	1	5	_____
D2267	Consumer Catalog	4	15	_____
D2268	Auto Rama Folder	0.50	2	_____
1962				
No number	The Big Ones Come from Gilbert		NRS	_____
D2277REV	Career Building Science Toys	8	25	_____
D2278	Dealer Catalog	2	12	_____
D2278REV	Revised Dealer Catalog	2	10	_____
D2282	Dealer Catalog		NRS	_____
D2283	HO Trains and Accessories	2	8	_____
D2307	Consumer Ad Mats		NRS	_____
D2310	Consumer Catalog	5	16	_____
M6874	Instruction Booklet	1	5	_____
1963				
D2321	Dealer Catalog	2	5	_____
D2321REV	Revised Dealer Catalog	5	15	_____
D2328	Consumer Catalog		NRS	_____
X863-3	Consumer Catalog	4	15	_____
1964				
X-264-6	Consumer Catalog	3	15	_____
No Number	Similar to X-264-6, 8 pages		NRS	_____
No Number	Similar to X-264-6, black binding		NRS	_____
564-11	Dealer Catalog	2	8	_____
1965				
X165-12	Dealer Catalog	7	15	_____
X165-12REV	Revised Dealer Catalog	7	15	_____
X365-10	Consumer Folder	2	5	_____
T465-5REV	Dealer Folder	1	3	_____
1966				
T-166-6	Dealer Catalog	4	10	_____
T166-7	Gilbert Action Toys	6	30	_____
X-466-1	Consumer Catalog	3	12	_____
M6788	All Aboard instructions	3	8	_____
1967*				
No number	Four-page Folder	1	5	_____

*Gilbert train production ended in 1966; however, an American Flyer Industries Folder was released for 1967.

ABBREVIATIONS

Pocket Guide Descriptions

AC	alternating current
bldgs.	buildings
B/W	bay window
comb.	combination
Cond	condition
DC	direct current
FP	diesel locomotive
gen.	generator
GP	diesel locomotive
Jct.	junction
KC	knuckle couplers
lett.	lettering
LH	left hand
(mv)	many variations
oper.	operating
PA	Alco diesel locomotive w/cab
pass.	passenger
PB	Alco diesel locomotive w/o cab
PM	Pike Master
ptd.	painted
QE	questionable existence
RC	remote control
REV	revised
RH	right hand
s-i-b	smoke in boiler
s-i-t	smoke in tender
sta.	station
S/W	square window
u	uncataloged
Wash.	Washington
West.	Western

Railroad Name Abbreviations

AF (AFL)	American Flyer (Lines)
ART Co.	American Refrigerator Transit Co.
ATSF	Atchison, Topeka and Santa Fe
B&A	Boston and Albany
BAR	Bangor and Aroostook Railroad
BM	Boston and Maine
BN	Burlington Northern
B&O	Baltimore and Ohio
C of G	Central of Georgia
CB&Q	Chicago, Burlington and Quincy
CMStP&P	Chicago, Milwaukee, St. Paul and Pacific
CN	Canadian National
CNJ	Central of New Jersey
CNW	Chicago North Western
C&NWRY	Chicago and North Western Railway
C&O	Chesapeake and Ohio
CP	Canadian Pacific
CRP	Central Railroad of Pennsylvania
D&H	Delaware and Hudson
DRG	Denver and Rio Grande
D&RGW	Denver and Rio Grande Western
DT&I	Detroit, Toledo, and Ironton
GAEX	General American Express
GM	General Motors
GM&O	Gulf, Mobile and Ohio
GN	Great Northern
HARR	Historic American Railroad
IC	Illinois Central
L&N	Louisville and Nashville
LNE	Lehigh New England
LV	Lehigh Valley
MEC	Maine Central
MKT	Missouri-Kansas-Texas
MP (MoPac)	Missouri Pacific
MR	Milwaukee Road
M&StL	Minneapolis and St. Louis
NASG	National Association of S-Gaugers
NH	New Haven
NKP	Nickel Plate Road
NP	Northern Pacific
NW	North Western
N&W	Norfolk and Western
NYC	New York Central
NYNH&H	New York, New Haven and Hartford
P&LE	Pittsburgh and Lake Erie
PC	Penn Central
PRR	Pennsylvania Railroad
REA	Railway Express Agency
RL	Reading Lines
RUT	Rutland
SF	Santa Fe
SP	Southern Pacific
T&P	Texas and Pacific
TCA	Train Collectors Association
TTOS	Toy Train Operating Society
UFGE	United Fruit Growers Express
UP	Union Pacific
USAF	United States Air Force
USM	United States Marines
VC	Vermont Central
WC	Wisconsin Central
WM	Western Maryland
WP	Western Pacific
WSX	White's Discount Centers

GREENBERG'S®
Great Train and Collectible Shows

Saturday 11 a.m. to 5 p.m. and Sunday 11 a.m. to 4 p.m.;
Two-day admission: $6 adults/$2 ages 6-12.

For more information about the Greenberg Show nearest you, send a SASE to Greenberg Shows, Inc., 7566 Main Street, Sykesville, MD 21784 or phone 410-795-7447, fax 410-549-2553, or visit our home page at www.greenbergshows.com. Changes may occur due to circumstances beyond our control.

— October through December, 1999 —

NORCROSS, GA *North Atlanta Trade Center*	**Oct. 2-3**
STONY BROOK, NY *State University of NY at Stony Brook*	**Oct. 9-10**
PENNSAUKEN, NJ *South Jersey Expo Center*	**Nov. 6-7**
MONROEVILLE, PA *Pittsburgh ExpoMart*	**Nov. 13-14**
EDISON, NJ *New Jersey Convention and Expo Center*	**Nov. 20-21**
NOVI, MI *Novi Expo Center ($6 incl p)*	**Nov. 20-21**
DANBURY, CT *O'Neill Ctr.,Western CT State Univ.*	**Nov. 27-28**
TIMONIUM, MD *Maryland State Fairgrounds*	**Dec. 4-5**
WILMINGTON, MA *Shriners Auditorium*	**Dec. 4-5**
FT. WASHINGTON, PA *Ft. Washington Expo Center*	**Dec. 11-12**
CHARLOTTE, NC *Charlotte Merchandise Mart*	**Dec. 18-19**
CLEVELAND, OH *Cleveland Convention Center*	**Dec. 18-19**

— January through August, 2000 —

NORCROSS, GA *North Atlanta Trade Center*	**Jan. 8-9**
VIRGINIA BEACH, VA *Virginia Beach Convention Center*	**Jan. 8-9**
JACKSONVILLE, FL *Greater Jacksonville Fairgrounds*	**Jan. 15-16**
LEBANON, PA *Lebanon Valley Expo Center*	**Jan. 15-16**
CHANTILLY, VA *Capital Expo Center*	**Jan. 22-23**
COLUMBUS, OH *Franklin County Veterans Memorial*	**Jan. 22-23**
TAMPA, FL *Florida State Fairgrounds*	**Jan. 22-23**
COLLINSVILLE, IL *Gateway Center*	**Jan. 29-30**
POMPAO BEACH, FL *The Omni, Broward Community College*	**Jan. 29-30**
FT. WASHINGTON, PA *Ft. Washington Expo Center*	**Feb. 5-6**
STONY BROOK, NY *State University of NY at Stony Brook*	**Feb. 12-13**
UPPER MARLBORO, MD *The Show Place Arena*	**Feb. 12-13**
NILES, OH *Eastwood Expo Center*	**Feb. 19-20**
MONROEVILLE, PA *Pittsburgh Expo Mart*	**Feb. 26-27**
PENNSAUKEN, NJ *South Jersey Expo Center*	**Mar. 4-5**
EDISON, NJ *New Jersey Convention & Expo Center*	**Mar. 11-12**
TIMONIUM, MD *Maryland State Fairgrounds*	**Mar. 18-19**
HACKENSACK, NJ *Fairleigh-Dickinson University*	**Mar. 25-26**
WILMINGTON, MA *Shriners Auditorium*	**Apr. 1-2**
MONROEVILLE, PA *Pittsburgh ExpoMart*	**July 8-9**
CHANTILLY, VA *Capital Expo Center*	**July 15-16**
PENNSAUKEN, NJ *South Jersey Expo Center*	**July 29-30**
TIMONIUM, MD *Maryland State Fairgrounds*	**Aug. 5-6**
EDISON, NJ *New Jersey Convention & Expo Center*	**Aug. 12-13**

Greenberg Auctions

All Greenberg auctions are held at the location below. The preview is at 8 a.m., and the auction at 9 a.m.

SYKESVILLE, MD *Sykesville-Freedom Fire Company*	**Oct. 9, 1999**
Community Building	**Apr. 8, 2000**
	July 8, 2000
	Oct. 14, 2000